"Children do say the da   e sayings will melt your heart and inspire your soul. A timeless book dedicated to parents and children everywhere."

— **Connie Dee, M.D., Pediatrician and Mother of two**

"Snapshots of Heaven is a must read for parents everywhere. Its joy-filled stories capture the beauty of children and their undeniable influence on our lives unlike any book I've ever read."

— **Dick Bruso, Founder, Heard Above the Noise**

"Michael, thank you for sharing your wonderful stories! I not only enjoyed them as a parent, but also as a second grade teacher. I know the potential of children as writers, and I am thrilled to tell you that I have shared several of your "snippets" of life to inspire my children as writers. They especially enjoyed, "The Shaving Cream Blizzard." Thanks again for sharing your gift of writing not only with me but with my 2nd grade students."

— **LeaAnn Allmendinger,**
  2nd grade teacher, Colorow Elementary, Colorado

"Michael Wells superbly captures the priceless joy our children bring us. My kids are grown now but the memories we shared are an indelible part of me. Wells's book brought back so much that we shared as a family; it also brought smiles and happy tears. Thank you."

— **David Weist, Deputy Chief/Administration (retired),**
  West Metro Fire Authority

"*Snapshots of Heaven* will touch your heart. You will love reading it and afterwards, keep it nearby. Then, on those days where it seems all your kids can do is have tantrums and make a mess, take this book off the shelf and open it to any page. Let it remind you of what really matters in life; and the joy and wonder that children bring to us."

— **Rita Emmett, author of**
  The Procrastinator's Handbook and The Procrastinating Child

"I am writing to you in regards to your excellent book, Snapshots of Heaven. I have had the opportunity to read your book and enjoy its wonderful anecdotes which are based on real-life experiences. As a school principal, I feel that the stories in your book can easily be incorporated in a teacher's daily planning – they offer not only an excellent opportunity to entertain our students but teach them valuable lessons. As a parent, I can honestly say that the book was inspirational and offered many moments of calm reflection, moments that are very necessary with our busy lifestyle."

> **– Nick Katalifos, Principal, General Vanier Elementary School**

"Snapshots of Heaven is a must read to help open the minds and hearts of everyone to one's personal experience of children and family. Thank you Michael."

> **– Father John E. Walsh, Roman Catholic Priest**

"An outstanding and unforgettable celebration of the special love we get from children."

> **– Pamela Papola, M.D., FAAP Developmental Behavioral Pediatrician and Mom**

"Recently my mother passed away after living with us for four years. My wife and I were the caregivers. I was home all the time with her, working out of the home. Our nineteen-year-old son took it extremely hard, and was home from college during the time of our bereavement. One night when he couldn't sleep, he asked, "Dad, what are you going to do now?" I said, "I'm finally all grown up now. Now it's your turn to take over and continue to do your best." Reading these stories that Michael Wells wrote made me smile, get teary, and remember all the wonderful times while growing up with the ongoing support and love from my parents. I treasure these times with our son now, as I always did throughout his childhood. To all parents: Cherish these moments with your children as times passes so quickly. Thank you Michael Wells for reminding us to love, to grow, to teach, and most of all to be grateful for the children in our lives."

> **– Randolph Williams, European Market Technologies**

"I strongly recommend this book. This collection of stories will transport you to those magical cherished moments we all have of our children. Guarantee to tickle your innards with lots of love and laughter. It reminds today's parents to be mindful; make time to listen and enjoy your children. They are a gift from God."

– Federico D. Western, Chief Warrant Officer 4(retired) U.S. Army, Father of five, Grandfather of three.

"Michael Wells gives all of us magic vision, letting us see eternity in a brief moment with a child."

– Rabbi Leigh Lerner

"I enjoyed reading the stories from *Snapshots of Heaven*. Many of these stories brought a smile to my lips, tears to my eyes, and warmth to my heart. As a parent of three young children, ages two, three, and six, these stories made me appreciate the time I do have with my children. I realized that someday, I too will look back on all these moments, whether happy, sad, or frustrating, and wonder how the time flew by so fast. I've learned that since we can't turn back the hands of time, we must cherish all the moments we have each and every day. Your book is an inspiration to all those fortunate enough to read it."

– Susan Chomar, Mother of three

"What a cool and heartwarming book! Michael Wells has paid a wonderful tribute to the love that children give us. If you're looking for a book to lift your spirits, this is it!"

– Gregory J.P. Godek, Author of *1001 Ways To Be Romantic*

"Having older teenage children as well as an eight-year-old has brought my life to many complications. I seem to have forgotten all the old snapshots of heaven that have been a part of my life. Your stories remind me that even though my life is at a more intense state now, I do need to remind myself of the precious moments I have been able to spend with my children. My kids are my heart and soul, and they are the source of my every breath, along with the love and support I get from my husband.

I'm sure if I think back in my mind I can put the present on hold and enjoy all my snapshots. You are doing a wonderful job with these stories and for someone like me it helps bring back the more important things in life, because life is too short."

–Loretta Mckeefery, Mother of three

SNAPSHOTS of HEAVEN®

40 FUNNY, PROFOUND,
REAL-LIFE STORIES ABOUT CHILDREN

MICHAEL WELLS

05 06 07 08 09 HH 5 4 3 2 1
First Edition
Printed in the United States of America
ISBN 10: 0-9737965-0-2
ISBN 13: 978-09737965-0-6
BISAC - FAM021000 Family & Relationships/Friendships
Library of Congress Control Number: 2005930377
$14.95 U.S. Funds

Cover design by Kathi Dunn, Dunn&Associates Design
Interior design by David Josephson, Cameo Publications, LLC.

Distributed through the services of Cameo Publications.

Dedication -

This book is dedicated to my own snapshots of heaven, my son, Jeremy, and my daughter, Jenna. Without the magic of your smiles and the thrill of your laughter, my heart would be lonely.

And to my wife Laure, whose smile makes the Mona Lisa ordinary. No poet, no writer, not even Mr. Shakespeare could articulate the words in my heart for you. No dictionary defines our love, only time. You are the guide of *Snapshots of Heaven*.

Contents

Contents

About the Author

Michael Wells is an author, entrepreneur, husband, and father of two. A lifelong resident of Montreal, Canada, he earned his bachelor's degree in psychology from Montreal's McGill University, where he wrote extensively for the university newspaper and local and regional publications.

After college, Michael launched a business all the while staying active in his children's lives. No matter what happened with the business, Michael always took great delight in the adventures and experiences he shared with his family, particularly all those times with his children and he wanted to document them.

He soon indulged his passion for writing and began preserving many of the experiences he and his family had over the years. As his book began to take shape, he shared his stories and ideas with others, and their enthusiastic reactions added fuel to an even greater vision that had begun to emerge. Not only did Michael want to share his own experiences with his children, but he also wanted to encourage and motivate adults everywhere to tell their stories of the little ones who "take them to heaven before their time."

As a member of the Montreal Chapter of the Canadian Association of Professional Speakers, Michael plans to carry his message to audiences everywhere, to aggressively pursue opportunities for radio and television interviews, and to relate, in future volumes, the stories of other parents, grandparents, uncles, aunts, and anyone else who has ever been caught in the magical spell of children.

The author and his American wife, Laure, have been married for 18 years, and are the parents of 15-year-old Jeremy and 13-year-old Jenna. Michael has played a very active role in the lives of his children, and has coached his son's hockey and soccer teams and his daughter's soccer teams for many years. Jeremy and Jenna have provided the many "snapshots of heaven" that Michael describes, in delightful detail in this book.

Acknowledgements

The great thing about writing is you know what you want to say, but you never know how it will come out or the discoveries you will make along the way. I began to write about children taking us to heaven and back before our time, and I quickly learned how so many share my vision and would go way beyond their lives to see that I made it to the finish line. A cast of a hundred good people re-visited their own stories while moving *Snapshots of Heaven* from an idle pipe dream to an exhilarating reality.

To David T., I don't know how to thank you. Once you grasped the potential of *Snapshots of Heaven*, you made it your mission to see me execute my dream. Never taking no for an answer, you are special and unique, I am glad you are my friend.

For Lawrence and Caryl, you guys have been with me almost from the beginning. Lawrence, you articulate smooth words like a dealer throws out cards, but the real you lives in that beautiful heart of yours. And to Caryl, whom I have known since high school, few have survived life's wars like you, and yet you are the trigger behind the question "what's next?" To know you is to understand life's rollercoaster and yet keep going. And thanks Suzanne for all the proofreading and help in the early stages of *Snapshots of Heaven*.

To my friends, Mike, Marla, Jon, Karyn, Ben, Renata, and Elliot, I love you guys for being there whenever I asked. Your patience astounds me, and your words of caring kept me going.

To Loretta and Lori-Ann, who passionately believed in *Snapshots of Heaven*. From day one, your passion and constructive feedback have helped shape the book. Thank you for your support.

To Ron Huza, Jonathon Sachs, and Bob Urichuck, thanks for selflessly giving so much of your time either by answering my never-ending emails or listening to me ask the same questions over and over again.

To my lawyer, Carol Desmond, who is not only a great trademark lawyer, but a dear friend and my own personal part-time psychiatrist.

And to Lew Cannizaro and his wife Maria who never told me they were too busy (even though they should have, considering the number of times I called on them for help).

To another one of my part-time "literary psychiatrists," Serena Williamson, thanks so much for telling me a thousand times (because once or twice is never enough with me) to get it done already.

To my dear spiritual friends, who have inspired and helped me throughout my literary quest: Father John Walsh, Rabbi Ron Cahanas, and Rabbi Leigh Lerner. Thank you.

To everyone at Cameo Publications, David and Dawn Josephson, Melinda Copp and Kimberly King, thanks for being so great at what you do. I hope the other authors you consult are not like me; otherwise you would need a specialist in Freudian psychiatry.

For Kathi Dunn, who designed an incredible book cover. You have my undying respect. And to Hobie, who gently navigated me each step along the way. Thanks.

And to Allison, who did so much to help me get to this point. What can I say? Working on *Snapshots of Heaven* has become everyone's dream, everyone's love. Week and after week, Allison, you rode the ride with me.

To be fair, the biggest break that dramatically moved *Snapshots of Heaven* to another level was my fortuitous meeting with Dick Bruso. After reading only a few stories and studying the primitive concept, Dick declared to me that I could not afford not to write *Snapshots of Heaven* and I owed it to the world to finish the gifts the book will bring so many people. When I took my first trip out to Denver to visit with you, I couldn't afford the cab fair to the airport, let alone everything else. Almost from the first shake of our hands, I felt as if I had known you forever and that you would play a critical role in my future. You are one of the rare teachers. In a world flooded with sharks, you kept me constantly focused on the priorities, never allowing me to stray (as I so easily can) with the counsel and firmness of a lifelong friend. Without you, *Snapshots of Heaven* would have died on the operating table years ago.

To my editor Bob Kelly, I have yet to meet you in person, but feel I know you better than many people I see almost every day. Thanks, Bob, for making the words from my heart readable to anyone who loves a kid more than life itself.

And to my friend Norine, your generous, detailed e-mail at five a.m. was, and is always, most appreciated.

To Craig De Souza, manager of the local Starbucks, thanks for the flowing words of kindness and the hand of support during some of the darkest days of my life. At a time when I measured my life by the lumps of sugar in your coffee, you alone, a total stranger, kept me sane until five.

And to the man who put his money where his mouth is. That solitary man who built a successful business, but never lost his humanity. That man of paradox, who shuns crowds but embraces life. Maybe it was timing for both of us; maybe it was luck. But whatever it was, your secret is safe with me. Your real strength is not your business prowess, but your heart. Thanks for making my dream your dream.

SNAPSHOTS
of HEAVEN®

Introduction

eaven's mirror can be seen through every child's eyes. If you want to, if you care enough, and if you let yourself go, you will feel heaven. Children write us real love letters, smother us with chocolate kisses, and surround our souls with hugs that take us to heaven and back before our time.

During the summer of 2001, my wife, Laure, and I took our kids, Jeremy and Jenna, on a family vacation to California. On those spectacular beaches, the unexpected happened. *Snapshots of Heaven* was born. What began as a usual family adventure to the beach, ended with a magic carpet ride around the moon and a chairlift to the stars. As I watched my kids run without a worry through the sand and seaweed, laughing and enjoying life without care, I could not only see, but also live what I had never lived before.

Children are really angels in disguise, teaching us lessons of love if we listen. The sad thing is most of us are too busy building our empires or fighting for the prize to even notice. To our surprise, just when we are planning the next trip to the park or adventure to the zoo, suddenly without warning, they turn fifteen and no longer want to go! We may shush them a hundred times to lessen their noise while they ride upon our shoulders, only to yearn twenty years later for one more shush.

As adults, when we end our day on the battlefield, after we've dealt with a thousand bottom lines, what probably matters most are the precious, fleeting moments we share with our children. They unlock our adult vault of cynicism and fears, and strip us of all our inhibitions. The initials of *Snapshots of Heaven* (S.O.H.) also mean children save our hearts every day. When we kiss them good night and close the lights, we rediscover why we work so hard.

In some inexplicable way, a child's magic seems to be their ability to bring us way back, to when we were like them and free. If God intended us to have a heart, children must have been the reason.

This book is the wakeup call we all need to cherish those treasures in our midst. It features forty funny, profound, real-life stories of children.

I hope you enjoy the book. More importantly, enjoy your own "Snapshots of Heaven." Hold them close. Laugh with them. Never stop saying, "I love you." And remember, while you laugh, while you play, and while you love, time is always waiting around the corner.

Write your Own Snapshot of Heaven

After each section in the book you will find a special place. Choose to glue a snapshot or just record your personal snapshot of heaven story.

Section One:
Everyday Lessons

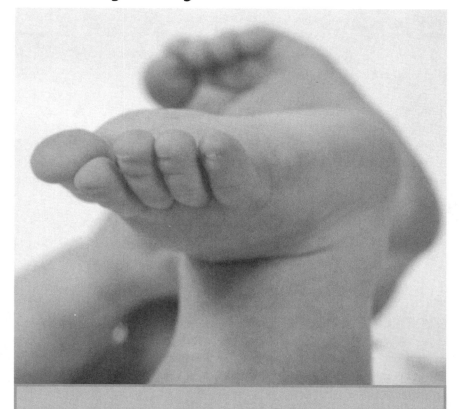

"Some of my best friends are children. In fact all of my best friends are children."

J. D. Salinger (1919-)

The Initiation

Having kids, they say, is easy. Almost anyone can do it. Raising kids, though—that's a whole different story! My wife Laure and I found this out very early, with our first child, Jeremy. When he was only six months old, we lived a harrowing night we'll never forget, but one that gave us our first real test of parenthood.

It was the first time we'd taken Jeremy to my in-laws' country house. At first, I wasn't sure if it was the right thing to do yet. "Maybe he's too young," I told my wife.

I'd have felt better if Laure's mother was going to be there, but she'd been delayed coming home from a trip. Now only her father was there, and men usually aren't as handy with babies as women are. So I was a bit apprehensive, but I realized my wife was right when she said I couldn't keep Jeremy in a bubble forever.

After Laure put Jeremy to bed, we were watching TV in the den, when I heard him start to cry loudly, almost as if he was out of control. His crying always made me nervous and, normally, Laure would convince me to leave him alone, as we didn't want to spoil him.

But this time she also got nervous and went to check on him. When she came back in the room with him, he was crying so violently his face had turned beet red. I never felt so utterly helpless in my life.

We'd been parents for just six months, and didn't have a clue what was wrong with our son. All we knew was that his crying was tearing at our hearts. Maybe it was just indigestion, but we were too green to know, and just too scared.

Laure's father suggested we take Jeremy next door to the lady who'd raised three boys. She'd know what to do. We were there in a flash, believing she'd give us the comfort we so desperately needed. Instead, she urged us to take Jeremy to the nearest hospital—which was sixty miles away!

"So much for raising three kids," I said to Laure. "Let's get going." As I raced down the highway, Jeremy kept crying and crying. All the way to the hospital, he never stopped.

It was 2:00 a.m. when we pulled up outside the emergency room. I let Laure off to race in with Jeremy, while I went to park the car. I couldn't believe how crowded the parking lot was. I said to myself, "Is everyone who's sick in the world here tonight? How long will my son have to wait?"

But he couldn't wait! The doctors would see this, of course, and check him right away. But when I reached the waiting room, I couldn't believe my eyes. There were at least twenty people ahead of us. I thought I'd scream.

Seeing my anguish, Laure ran over, saying, "Calm down, calm down. They took his temperature and it's normal. They think it's only indigestion. We'll just have to wait. They don't think it's serious."

"But do they know for sure?" I asked her.

"No, of course not."

"Great, Laure, great! They're playing medical jeopardy with our son. They don't know, do they?"

"Calm down," she said again.

I sat down, got a cup of coffee, and just watched our son cry and cry and cry.

Then, the next thing I knew, Laure was waking me. "It's time to go," she announced.

"What? What time is it?"

"It's 5:00 a.m."

"How's Jeremy?"

"He's fine. He fell asleep."

"Did the doctors ever see him?"

"No."

"So what happened?"

"Nothing."

"What was wrong with him?"

"I don't know. But he's been sleeping for the last hour. And you've been asleep from the moment we got here. Someone had to stay awake," she added. "Besides, you drove here and you were a nervous wreck. You needed the rest. Now it's my turn. Jeremy and I are sleeping while you drive back."

On the way, I took my time. For the first time in my life, time became my friend. And, like a good friend, it stood still and silent, allowing me to live my moment. Not a soul was on the road. Summer's gift to the world, its sunrise, was slowly raising its sleepy head above the mountains. It was a beautiful sight.

But there would be other sunrises to see, so I turned to take a quick look at my son peacefully sleeping in Laure's arms, realizing I was the luckiest man on earth. I had a son to raise and I couldn't wait. My initiation into parenthood was complete.

The Shaving Cream Blizzard

I t was five o'clock on a bitter cold morning in January 1995. My son Jeremy was about to reach the age of five. The fact that he wasn't awake yet, yelling or tearing the house apart, astonished me, so I decided I'd better check on him. At that hour, his room was still dark, except for the tiny nightlight beside the door.

When I put out my hand to turn it off, I felt this thick foamy substance, as if globs of what felt like shaving cream had dropped from the ceiling onto my hand. I said to myself in disbelief, "This can't be. I'm imagining things."

I immediately realized I needed to see if my son was okay so, for some strange reason, I knelt down and began crawling cautiously to his bed. I had no idea what to expect. As I got there, I decided to lie next to my little hurricane for a few precious moments before he woke up.

The second my body hit his bed, I started to slip and slide out of control. What was going on? I had to find out. As I jumped up and turned on his light, I could hardly believe my eyes. Next to the bed was a long mirror, showing Jeremy, me and the entire room covered in layers of shaving cream.

I didn't know whether to laugh or cry. Then before I could answer myself, I slipped to the ground, falling into mountains of shaving cream.

I never knew I had so much of the stuff. When, or rather how, did my little son do all this? There was shaving cream everywhere—on his sheets, his pajamas, the walls, the curtains, his toys, and the carpet.

The most amazing thing was that Jeremy, who never slept, who had more energy than five nursery schools, was sound asleep, with a big smile on his face. It was if he was telling me, "Welcome to parenthood, Pops."

This was my first bizarre experience as a father, an unexplainable chapter in a forever story. I didn't remember reading about shaving cream in any of the parent books I'd read. Maybe I missed that chapter.

What should I do? Was this a test? My first real test as a father and teacher? Then before I could answer my own questions, Jeremy opened his eyes and blurted out, "What do you think, Daddy? Did I do good? Is it enough for us to have fun?"

"What are you talking about, Jeremy? All I see is enough shaving cream for the whole world in one room."

"What do you mean, Daddy? What's shaving cream?"

"The stuff daddy uses every morning on his face."

"This is snow, Daddy, not shaving cream. Yesterday I saw you were upset because you said there wasn't enough snow outside yet for us to make a snowman. And I know you don't like the cold."

"How do you know that, Jeremy?"

"Because you're always shaking when it's cold outside. The picture on the cans in the kitchen shows a mountain of snow. Now you can make a snowman without going out in the cold."

I started to ask him what cans, but then I caught myself. "Oh no, Jeremy," I said, and then I hugged him, both of us swimming in shaving cream. What a hilarious sight!

It all came back to me. Last night, when I stopped at the store, there was a special on shaving cream, so I stocked up. When I got home, I left the cans on the kitchen table.

For the next two hours, before my wife woke up, Jeremy and I used every paper towel in the house to clean up his room. We never told Laure.

As the years flew by, there were hundreds of other nights and days like that one. Only now they become more complicated, more serious. What does a parent say when trying to teach his kid the difference between right and wrong? What are the words he'll hear and learn from? Will your lesson in life push him away, or will he hug you more for speaking from the heart?

I've learned every situation is different, and every act demands a different message. But the lesson the indoor blizzard taught me was that while your heart and mind search for what to do and say, never forget who you're talking to. It's your kid, and once upon a time, all he wanted to do was build a snowman with you.

True Heroes

It's just a little kiss on the cheek – but I never have enough of them. It's just four words – "I love you, Daddy" – but they make my heart sing. It's just a brief caress on my face – to see if I've shaved today – but it's a touch of heaven. It's just a short phone call – to tell me where they are – but I hang up happy. It's just a voice mail – reminding me to have a good day – but it makes my day.

These everyday, simple things my kids and I do will never be featured on the Evening News, nor will any reporters come calling. It's not something we talk about; it's something we do. The reward isn't money, fame, or power. It's not the Pulitzer Prize, nor the Nobel Prize. There's no Olympic gold, silver, or even bronze to be won.

Laure and I, like millions of parents around the world, are the silent, anonymous soldiers of love who are never ready for the ultimate responsibility—having kids. We hear the stories, watch the movies, read the books, and listen to the "experts" who tell us all the secrets and rewards of raising children. But, with all that information, we're still not ready. Raising kids is strictly on-the-job training.

With every day that passes, I learn more and more that it doesn't matter if you're the President of the United States, or the CEO of a major corporation, the biggest—and I mean the biggest—responsibility anyone ever faces in life is raising a healthy, happy, and confident child. That's the real prize!

But it's no easy feat in today's world, where faster is better and more is never enough. Patience is at a premium. Technology has its good and bad features, sometimes leading the way, sometimes leading us astray.

In all the centuries the world has existed, there is to me no greater challenge than today's parents struggling to see their kids be happy. I've learned that the moods my kids are in are the thermometer of my life. When they're laughing themselves silly, I'm hot and ready to take on the universe. When they're sad, I'm cold and frustrated by not having all the answers.

As a family, we've seen the beaches of Cape Cod, the great monuments of Washington, D.C., and the New York skyscrapers that touch the clouds. We've traveled throughout the breathtaking state of California and went on every ride in the "happiest place on earth" – Disneyland! But as my kids get older, I see nothing that compares to the simple day-to-day things we do together. It's the glue that bonds us— the reason I go on.

And wherever I go, whatever my kids and I do together, whether we walk, drive, bike, or rollerblade, I see hundreds of other parents doing the same things. They're the true heroes of our time, who stand with their kids through the sunshine and through the storm, true heroes who know they need no Nobel Prize, no Olympic gold.

They're already here. They can go to the podium every day. All they have to do is open their arms to receive the greatest rewards in the world.

Bless You, Mr. Bell

F or one week, twice a year, Las Vegas becomes the center of the men's apparel universe. The great, humongous "Magic Show," billed as the convention of conventions, is in full swing. Imagine an area where hundreds of Boeing 747s are assembled side by side, reaching as far as the eye can see. Only in this case, all the big name clothing and accessory companies in the world are there instead of 747s.

It's my first Magic Show, and I'm excited. People come from all over the world, buyers and sellers, searching for the next opportunity. Like me, they're all hoping to make it worthwhile. And don't let the smiles and laughter fool you—everyone's deadly serious. Nobody says what he really thinks. It's business—strictly business!

My excitement is mixed with some apprehension. Usually I'm only away for a day or so; this would be almost a week. And, whenever I travel, I always call home at least twice a day, morning and night, to see how my family is doing.

I always try to keep up with my kids' school life. I need to know when their exams are. What's their favorite subject? Who's their fa-vorite teacher? Are they having fun, and learning a lot of cool things? Whenever we talk, whether I can see their eyes or I'm three thousand miles away, I feel like the parent reporter, listening to them, writing their every word in my mind, feeling their every expression in my heart.

When my kids talk about their days, it's almost as if we're meeting for the first time. The smile on my face could circle the world, just listening to them go on and on. Honestly, I don't remember a lot of what they say. But who cares? It doesn't matter. They love talking and I love listening, wherever I am.

I always thought I was the only one who anxiously waited for this daily ritual with my kids, devouring every word like a man starved for some meaning to life. One minute, I'm this guy who, like many others, leaves every morning, clothed in this invisible armor, with my invisible sword in hand, ready to do battle with the invisible enemies I meet everyday. In another instant, changing faster than Superman in the phone booth, I hear my kids and melt.

But I learned something in Las Vegas. Working fifteen-hour days for nearly a week taught me I wasn't alone. Maybe I always knew this. Maybe every parent knows this. We all needed to hear our kids talk about their day when we're there, or hear about it when we're away.

At 5:00 p.m. Vegas time, 8:00 p.m. back east (where many of the participants come from), and near suppertime in the west, the real Magic Show begins. Suddenly, it seems every cell phone throughout the more than 100,000 square feet of convention space is on its most important call of the day. These tough, driven men and women suddenly burst out uncontrollably in childlike sounds. To hear them talk to their little ones is quite an experience.

Would the real tough business owner stand up? "So what did you do today, Danny?" "How was the park, Laura?" "Did you enjoy piano, Susie?" "Was karate fun, Michael?" "What was that, Benji? You went to the toilet, good boy!" "Mommy loves and misses you very much. I'll be home soon, Brandon." "Let Daddy speak to Mommy now."

I can't believe my eyes and ears. What a show is going on! It's the real show, the real deal. The real wheeling and dealing is going on through cell phones of every shape, size, and color. And all are connected to one customer, one location—called HOME!

An atmosphere of quiet serenity pervades the normally hectic and noisy convention halls—a mood of such contentment, that I stand there stunned. Never have I witnessed this before. Every night it's the same routine. Like clockwork. During the day, we're moving at the speed of light, wheeling and dealing, buying and selling, giving Academy Award-type performances.

Then, right at 5:00 p.m., the transformation takes place. The pace slows, and the cell phone becomes our only contact with the loved ones who make up our real world. The cell is the technological marvel that allows us to complete the day with a smile and recharge for tomorrow.

Some 125 years earlier, in another convention hall, a twenty-nine-year-old man is about to demonstrate his new invention. As the voice of Alexander Graham Bell, speaking from another room, reaches the exhibit hall, there's pandemonium—the telephone is born! "The day is coming," the young inventor predicts, "when...friends will converse with each other without leaving home."

You were so right, Mr. Bell—and not just friends, but families too. God bless you, Mr. Bell! And, by the way, in case you're listening, thank you for the cell!

Goodnight Kisses

I t had been an all-too-typical day at work. Frustration! Battles! Everything that could go wrong did. Every time I tried to leave, something else fell on my desk. Why does it always seem that when you're just about to leave the day seems to start? The phone calls, good and bad, pour in as you're about to shut down your computer—the aggravating end to an aggravating day.

Then, if all this wasn't enough, I got the call I'd been dreading for months. My friend Rickie, whom I've known since we were ten, asked me when I could come and visit him. He'd just gone back into the hospital and didn't think he'd be going home.

"How long did the doctor say, Rickie?" I foolishly asked.

"Quick, very quick," he answered. Then he asked me the most impossible question I've ever been asked. "Why me? I'm only thirty-nine years old? I have two beautiful children. What's going to happen to them?"

I felt stupid. I didn't know what to say. What could I say?

"So, are you coming?" he asked again. "When? Don't tell me soon. I don't have soon."

"Today's Monday, Rickie. I'll see you this week."

"Promise?"

"Of course."

"Okay. See you then. Oh, by the way," he went on, "one more thing."

"Yes? What is it?" I asked, not knowing what in the world he could possibly add to the conversation at this point.

"How are Jenna and Jeremy?"

"They're okay." I didn't know what to say. Again, I felt so stupid so utterly useless. "They're fine," I said, "thanks for asking."

"Gotta go now," he said. "I'm getting tired."

As soon as I hung up, my wife called. "Don't ask," I said. "I'm going for a bite to eat. I'll tell you all about it when I get home."

"Okay." That was all she said, realizing something was up.

I could have gone right home, but I needed what my wife called "my PT," my private time. After this day, I needed months of PT, but that wasn't in the cards. I drove around the neighborhood thinking about my day, and especially about my friend Rickie. "Why him?" I asked. "Why him?"

I drove into my driveway and slowly made my way into the house. "You look a wreck," was all my wife could say. I wasn't upset by her words because that's exactly how I felt. She was right again and only meant it because she cared. I knew that.

I told Laure every awful detail of my day, and in particular, the part about Rickie, and how we both were going up to see him the next weekend, probably for the last time. Then, in my typical way, I quickly changed the subject and asked her something I'd been meaning to ask her for months.

"Do the initials for Snapshots of Heaven (SOH) ever remind you of SOS, the distress signal? They're very similar."

She didn't say a word, but just gave me one of those "I can't believe you said that" looks.

"Don't they?" I asked.

"No, they don't," was her direct reply. "SOH is better, much better."

"How so?" I asked

"It stands for Save Our Hearts, and that's what our kids do. They save our hearts – everyday!"

For perhaps the first time all day, I smiled. She was right, of course. I didn't say a word. I knew exactly what I had to do next.

I went to see my kids, who'd already been asleep for awhile. I stood there staring at them, and I melted. Then I bent over and kissed them goodnight on their cheeks. They were so soft that I couldn't stop kissing them. In a flash that made everything okay, or at least bearable.

Laure was right. The pain and wounds of the day were instantly healed by these two little heroes, ages five and seven.

My friend Rickie died a short time later. After I got the news, I told Jeremy that Daddy had lost a good friend. "Where did he go?" Jeremy asked.

"To heaven," I said. "To heaven, Jeremy."

Then he ran over and hugged me and, for a second, just a second, I thought it was my friend Rickie saying goodbye. Now I understood what Laure meant when she said that SOH stands for "Save Our Hearts." That's what kids do. They save our hearts every day. I just looked up and said, "Goodbye, Rickie. Goodbye, my friend."

The Soccer Star

Jenna never seemed to take to sports the way Jeremy did. By the time she was eight, I felt enough was enough. I always felt soccer was a game she could be good at, if she only tried. I decided the only way to get her to try was to play with her, or do the next best thing, coach her. So when I proposed that she sign up for soccer the next spring, and that I'd coach her, she jumped at the chance.

Way before May rolled around, with snow still on the ground, Jenna insisted I take her out and practice, but who played soccer in the Arctic? Almost every weekend, we went to the park, shoveled the snow away, and practiced. Jenna just wanted to start the soccer season early and I had to oblige. After all, what coach is going to discourage an eager player?

Finally, the season began. Jenna didn't know the rules, so I had to teach her, and repeat every step along the way. We lost the first two games. But then I noticed something. Jenna came away from each game laughing and asking me when the next game was scheduled. Win or lose, she really didn't care. She just wanted to be with me and have fun.

"Aren't we having fun, Daddy? Aren't we?" We were. But I've always been a very competitive guy. I loved to win. I didn't have to win every game. But I didn't enjoy losing every one either. I confess

I didn't know what to expect when I started the season, but I certainly didn't expect this. We were a disaster! And everyone was having so much fun, except me.

It was a short season, thankfully lasting only eight weeks. Midway through the season, Jenna had improved a lot and comfortably found her position at defense, where she displayed a lot of promise. The whole team had improved a lot. But they didn't seem to care. They were having the time of their lives.

The last weekend finally arrived, and we still had yet to win one game. At least the girls were consistent. But our last game was against the first place team. I prayed for rain, but the day turned out to be beautiful. The referee blew the whistle and immediately the other team scored. This was going to be a long game, I thought.

Then, to my shock, we scored three minutes later. I couldn't believe it. The game was actually tied. I rubbed my eyes. Maybe I had to wake up. Then we scored again. What was going on here? Was this our team? Or was I temporarily transported to another city? On both goals, Jenna got an assist.

She was playing great. Nobody could get past her. Our goalie was making saves I never knew she could. We were actually playing like a team.

Halftime came with the score still 2-1 for us. But I was sure the fairy tale would soon end. And I was right. In less than five minutes of the second half, they scored two goals. Down by one, with one minute left, I felt it was over.

Just at that moment, the ball landed on Jenna's foot. "Kick, Jenna, kick with all your might to Nancy (our best shooter). Kick like you want to hit the sun." And kick she did!

Wow! The ball went in between their players, landing a few feet from Nancy. "Don't miss, Nancy," I yelled. "Don't miss! Kick, Nancy! Smack it in!" And she did.

I couldn't believe it. We tied the best team in the league. What a game! What a finish! I ran onto the field and started rolling in the grass like a five-year-old. The girls were jumping so hard I thought they would lose their breath. We tied, but against this team, it was a victory. What fun!

The season was over. We never won a game. But I no longer cared—and that was a first for me. Just to have fun and to love what you do had never been enough. I had to win. I thought if I didn't win, I lost. Then Jenna and the rest of the girls opened my eyes and heart to an experience I never had before and never dreamed possible. Play with passion. Love what you do. Have fun. That's much more important than a bunch of trophies gathering dust on the mantle. This is what they taught me. And they were only eight years old.

The Wake-up Call

I t was a crazy time in my life. My business was going full blast and I was going even faster. As much as I loved my kids, I was consumed by my work. Boy, did I have a lot to learn, and didn't even know it. Little did I know the coming weekend would be the wake-up call of my life.

As usual, my wife Laure had to practically drag me on a three-day family vacation to Lake George, New York, to visit an amusement park called "The Great Escape." Laure had made all the plans, but didn't believe I was coming until the car actually left our house with me in it.

The drive down was easy, and my cell phone didn't ring once. But the truth is I'd timed it that way. It was a long weekend holiday and we left on a Saturday. Most of our family trips had been planned this way, around holidays and weekends. I rarely took a weekday off, but if I did, I was on my phone constantly, to the point that Laure and I would get into an argument about it, making us all miserable. For a smart guy, I was pretty stupid—but the worst was yet to come.

It was really hot at Lake George, and The Great Escape was the best place to be. We were having the time of our lives. Before we knew it, however, it was eight o'clock, and the park would be closing in an hour.

I ran back to the car for some towels, but when I reached into my bathing suit pocket for my car keys, they weren't there! I suddenly started to panic. What was I going to do? How would we get home? And even worse, my house and office keys were on the same chain.

Frantically, I ran back to the water park, to the ride where I believed I'd lost my keys. Ironically, it was a gentle, slow-moving ride where you lie on large tubes as you circle the park. I presumed my keys had fallen out of my pocket while I was lying on one of them.

When I couldn't spot my keys in the water, I grew more anxious, so I jumped in without a mattress, which was strictly forbidden. In seconds, two big burly guys jumped in and grabbed me. Hustling me out of the water, they held me until Tom, the park's supervisor, arrived.

"What do you think you're doing?" he demanded. "You could get arrested for what you did, or thrown out of the park indefinitely." Then he saw I was hurting and that something was wrong.

"What's the problem?" he asked. I told him I'd done a very stupid thing, that I'd lost my keys and needed to find them right away. As I babbled on, he suggested I calm down, and offered to help.

About this point, Laure and our kids, Jenna and Jeremy, came running toward me. They'd heard about a big commotion and came back to see what was going on. Laure also told me to calm down, but I wasn't listening. Then Tom said, "As soon as the park closes, I'll have our staff jump in the water with you and help find your keys. If they're not too small, they won't go through the filter vents and, in that case, there's a good chance we'll find them."

For the next hour, I was on pins and needles but, finally, 9:00 p.m. arrived, and the big sweep began, with more than fifty of us combing every inch of the area. I was so emotional you'd think we were looking for someone, not something.

A half-hour later, Tom handed me my keys. I'll never forget his words. "I have three kids of my own," he said. "Do yourself a favor, and next time remember it's only keys. If you lost anyone behind you (pointing to my family), you'd have a real loss. The rest is just stuff. Look at you. Look what this did to you. If you don't mind me saying so, I suggest you wake up, for your health and theirs." Then he shook my hand and wished me well.

My kids and Laure rushed to hug me. Their unspoken message was, "We're what really matters, not some silly keys. Get your priorities straight."

Lake George was a big wake-up call to my heart. Unfortunately, it took years for me to hear it. I should have heard the alarm ring a long time ago. Tonight was a test and I'd failed. And it had nothing to do with losing some keys. The worst part was having my kids see their father lose control over something so relatively minor. Next time, I'll think twice about the kind of example I'm setting for them, because what they see is far more important than what I say.

The Chiclet Man

I said the eulogy for my grandfather's funeral. Harry had said he was eighty-nine but who knows? In 1905, when he came as a boy from Russia, a birth certificate wasn't included. So, eighty-nine, eighty-five, ninety-two, who cared?

In a eulogy, you're supposed to remind the world what the person's achievements were. Harry was a simple, decent man whose achievement in life was just that. Did anybody notice? Did anybody care? When you give eulogies, you never know. It's not like you face thunderous applause, or even a chorus of boos.

As I spoke, my eyes focused on my kids, Jenna and Jeremy, ages nine and eleven. It was their first experience attending a funeral. I knew they loved their only great grandfather so much, and I thought it was time they came. I had no idea what to expect, but I knew they should be there.

We never talked about the funeral until a year later, when it was time to unveil Harry's tombstone and officially bury him. In fifteen minutes it was over, after a few prayers, a few choice last words, and a lot of tears. Harry was officially gone.

I hustled my kids back into the car. Again, there was a strange silence. This wasn't normal, I thought. Something had to be done. They were never quiet. I couldn't let this be the exception, despite the situation. But what to say? Finally, Jenna came to my rescue.

"Daddy, what did the first number mean on Grandpa's grave?"

"That was the year he was born."

"So what did the last number mean?"

"That's the year he died, Jenna."

"Do people always do that, Daddy?"

"Yes," I told her.

"Then where's the rest?" she asked

I hesitated. "What do you mean, Jenna?" knowing exactly what she meant.

"Well, they drew a line, Daddy, between the numbers."

"You mean the dash, Jenna?"

"Yes. Why?"

"Why what?"

"You know, why the dash? What does it mean?"

I told Jenna the truth, at least as far as I knew it. "I don't know, I really don't know, Jenna. I guess it's always been that way, so they just continue doing it."

"But if they write when he was born and when he died, why don't they write a short story or poem about how he lived? What he did. Who he married. His kids. All that kind of stuff, Daddy. You know what I mean?"

"Yes, I know, Jenna." But I really didn't have an answer.

"And the dash, Daddy, it's so, so…"

"What, Jenna?"

Then my son Jeremy spoke. "So nothing, Daddy. It's nothing! Grandpa wasn't nothing. You said it yourself in the speech you gave. You said he was a great man who helped people."

Jenna wouldn't let up. "Does everyone have a dash, Daddy?"

"Yes, everyone."

"So why do they all have a dash? Isn't it important what they did in between those numbers?"

"Yes, of course, Jenna."

"I think for Grandpa, he should have Chiclets instead of the dash, since he loved them so much," said my son.

"I think he should have a smiley face, since he was always smiling," suggested Jenna.

Unburdened by adult traditions, Jenna and Jeremy unleashed a lost, hidden treasure chest of thoughts in me. I started to think about what they said. They were right. Why the dash? It meant nothing. Was it only to be brief? To the point? To represent someone's life?

Then, finally, I understood what my kids were talking about. It wasn't about Chiclets, and it wasn't about smiley faces. My kids got it right away. Harry, more than most people, had lived his life from the heart.

As we got near home, Jenna asked me to stop at her favorite candy store. She was running low and wanted to stock up. Inside, she was taking her usual forever and I, as usual, was growing impatient. My daughter could never decide about the smallest things.

As the man was adding up the costs, Jenna became frantic as always, finding it impossible to decide what to leave in and what to leave out. Then she pointed to the bottom of the counter and smiled. "Look, Daddy. Chiclets! The yellow kind. Grandpa's favorite. Let's buy some, Daddy."

"But you don't like Chiclets, Jenna."

"C'mon, Daddy, let's do it for Grandpa."

Now, every time Jenna and I go to a candy store, we buy yellow Chiclets. Neither of us cares much for them. But Jenna thinks every time we buy some, it makes Harry smile. And who am I to argue? After all, she was nine, while I was way past forty.

The Best Sound in the World

eep Beethoven. Never mind Louis Armstrong, The Beatles, or
The Stones. Sure they were all great but, after all, it's still only
music. The best sound in the world has nothing to do with any
of the great composers or musicians. No, the best sound in the
world comes from my den where, almost every Sunday afternoon, Jenna
and Jeremy are laughing so loud you can hear them all over the house.

It's 12:45. We've finished lunch and it's time for Dad's Car Service
to get rolling again. "Jenna, it's time to go to dance school." I yell, trying to make myself heard above the laughter. "Does anyone hear me?"
I'd just come back from picking Jeremy up at basketball, and now it's
time to don the chauffeur cap again. Going and coming. Coming and
going. It seems that's all I do on Sunday. Jenna continues to ignore me,
or can't hear me, as she and Jeremy are now going full blast on the
karaoke.

I think Paul McCartney would have been proud, hearing the pas-
sions my kids put into "Yellow Submarine." Over and over again, they
stomp their feet, clap their hands and go into a frenzy whenever the
chorus comes on, their bodies moving to the music like circus acrobats.
"We all live in the yellow submarine, we all live in the yellow submarine."

Then, Jenna jumps up, pretending she's on stage in front of thousands of fans, laughing and singing wildly at the same time. I melt as I watch the show. Carnegie Hall couldn't come close to this one. Every note is a showstopper, every laugh is applause, and every smile brings the house down.

What an indescribable sight! Jeremy's rolling on the couch in a fit of uncontrollable laughter, while Jenna prances up and down like a ten-year-old Britney Spears. Finally, my daughter comes back to earth. "So, Daddy," she says, "are you taking me to dance school? You told me fifteen minutes ago we had to leave in five minutes. We'll be late if we don't hurry. So are we going?"

"Yes, yes, yes, we're going. Jenna."

"When, Daddy? It's almost one. What time does my class start?"

"1:15," I reply.

"Okay, so we should go now. Right, Daddy?"

"Right, Jenna!"

On the way to the dance hall, Jenna shows me a CD in her hand with music by one of her favorite singers, called Pink. I can't believe it, but in the picture, Pink really had pink hair. "She wasn't born with pink hair, Daddy," explains Jenna, with a smile that sends my heart soaring.

"I know," I answer with a smile. "Why did you bring the CD, Jenna?"

"Everyone in the dance class has to bring their own music, Daddy."

"You know," she continues, just as we drive up to the dance hall, "I feel so alive." Then, she throws open the car door, reminds me to pick her up in an hour, and goes running like the wind into the dance hall, the sound of her girlish laughter trailing behind her. I don't even get my kiss on the cheek. And I don't even get to answer her.

"I feel so alive too, Jenna," I say to the wind. "Thanks to you and your brother for your laughter, the best sound in the world, I feel so alive, too!"

How Was Your Day, Daddy?

For almost twenty-five years, I traveled a thousand miles an hour, diligently building my business, in search of freedom from the demands of others. After all those years, my business became a trap. Instead of being liberated, I became a prisoner. Though I had a partner, the business finally did me in and I lost it, going bankrupt.

I guess everyone, one day, be it personal or professional, meets his or her Waterloo. My experience taught me it's true. In order to live, you have to die. But I also learned that with the magic presence of your children, who are oblivious to disaster, you don't die.

Children don't understand extreme joy or extreme grief. They realize something's wrong, but unlike adults it's never the end of the world. In this sense, they possess magical powers that we lose as we age.

Without a word from me, Jenna and Jeremy knew something was wrong when I met my Waterloo. But their smiles never changed. In fact, their faces seem brighter than ever, as if they were trying to send me a message. It was as if they were saying, "Follow us, Daddy, we'll lead the way." And lead the way they did.

After several months of wandering, I finally got a job. As soon as I received the news, I became excited, very excited. But nothing, absolutely nothing, would prepare me for what waited for me when I came home after my first day. Without hesitation, Jenna and Jeremy, like angels darting from the gates of heaven, ran to give me a hug, and with five simple words, "How was your day, Daddy?" propelled me on a new destiny.

With their arms around my neck, and a hundred kisses later, they dissolved my heartache. Whatever pain I was enduring, or however dismal I thought my future, Jenna and Jeremy abruptly woke me up with their hugs and kisses. Their actions melted my heart and cleared the fog in front of me. To fight back, you need something to fight for. As obvious at this seems, it doesn't hit you until you have to fight.

In all my adult life, I'd never worked for somebody else. So this was a momentous day, in more ways than one. Without even taking off my coat, we sat around the kitchen just discussing how my day was. Many times, I've talked to my kids. Many times, we've laughed together over every subject you could think of. But nothing, absolutely nothing, pierced my heart more than my kids' words on this day. And never was it more needed. On this day, even the best Harvard Medical School graduates couldn't come close to the medicine of my kids. None knew better what to do than they did. And the best part was that it was real!

What I thought would be one of my most difficult days turned out to be unforgettable. That's the great thing about life; it's a surprise, a long or short surprise. They can be good or bad surprises. But anything can happen at anytime, and does.

There's no formal invitation. Life doesn't care if it's black tie or blue jeans. Bang, the ferocity of life hits you. As with a winter storm in July, you're never ready. I understood at the end of this day that life was unpredictable – but my kids weren't. The force of their love prevailed over any hell I entered. Their words were the messengers of their love.

All I had to do was take the time and listen. And I did. We went on for over an hour, talking about my day, talking about their day. It was quite a moment. Again, it seemed only a moment. By the end, they had me laughing more than I expected to. All of a sudden, a deep peace covered me. I felt so blissful.

I was lost in the fog of their words. Who cared? What a first day! Was this, I thought to myself, a pattern of days to come? The strange scene was the beginning of my new life. Yes, I had lost a lot, but perhaps, in some inexplicable way, I had gained something that would take months, maybe years, to understand. I was on a new road.

To myself, I wondered why now? Why, in all these years since they learned to talk, they never asked me, even once, how my day was? When it began, I felt as though I was falling off a cliff. Then somebody sent me a parachute. And the parachute, I knew, was Jenna and Jeremy.

The Giggles

It was a spontaneous eruption of laughter that would have made Mt. Vesuvius look tame. My daughter Jenna and her friend Kira burst into such an uncontrollable cloudburst of giggling that I think even the heavens joined in. If giggles were bubbles, the whole world would have been in danger of drowning in a sea of soap.

It was Saturday evening. Jenna, Kira, my wife Laure, and the kids' grandmother—Mamie Rose, as they'd called her from birth— were playing a serious game of Scrabble. Well, it was as serious as you can get with two eleven-year-old girls. For nearly two hours all was quiet and serene. I was peacefully watching TV in the next room, oblivious to the "Game of the Century," taking place in the kitchen.

Then the heavenly craziness started, slowly at first but quickly gathering steam. First, I heard my daughter start to lose it; then Kira joined in. At this point, Laure and Mamie Rose tried everything in their adult power to calm them down, so they could finish the game. After all, *The New York Times* was probably going to call any minute for an interview on the outcome of this global event.

I jumped up and joined the adult side, urging the girls to be still. I couldn't hear my movie. I was serious—deadly serious. I wanted to watch my movie, and that's all I cared about. Laure and Mamie Rose wanted to finish the game and that's what they cared about.

After saying my piece, I went back to my movie, thinking I'd calmed the storm. But it didn't last long. Instead of stopping, the giggles were getting louder. The whole affair was running out of control. I made a second try for quiet, but something told me I was losing ground. I still had the support of the ladies, but the looks on their faces weren't as stern as they'd been earlier. Whose side were they on? I made it clear I wanted to watch my movie without any more noise.

Just when I was convinced my message was received, the sound of the giggles went up a few notches. I couldn't believe it. Wasn't anybody listening to me? Was I talking to an empty room? For a moment, I questioned myself.

But, enough was enough. I was close to my boiling point. This was supposed to be my little time of escape—relaxation—watching a movie. Was that asking too much? Was I being selfish? No, not at all, I concluded.

Having settled that matter, I decided to storm into the kitchen this time and finish the job I'd started earlier. But as I entered the room, I stopped dead in my tracks. Not only were Jenna and Kira still rolling on the floor giggling, with tears streaming down their cheeks, but my wife and Mamie Rose had joined the ride. It was an incredible sight.

What could I do? I watched in disbelief, my mind going a million miles a second. Then it hit me – the answer to one of the great mysteries of life. Why, especially, do kids giggle? Kids' giggles were invented for a reason. And now I knew why.

Somewhere, many centuries ago, someone understood that we adults needed a real break from it all. We need to escape through this secret tunnel, just for a little while, to remember what it was like, and what it can be like again. To remind us what not to lose, and to hang on, with all our adult might and power, to magic. All we need, once in awhile, is to go through the Tunnel of Giggles. And the only guide is a kid.

That night the tunnel opened wide for all of us, including me. Within minutes, I joined the ruckus. How could I not? What movie? Who cared? That night I understood the power of Jenna's giggles. They were ordinary giggles that became anything but ordinary when my daughter and her friends got rolling. That night reminded me there's no such word in any children's dictionary as "ordinary." That night I saw only an extraordinary sight.

The Giggles

Hearing Jenna's giggles, seeing her power taking the other adults back, way back, if only for an hour or so, to when they were kids, amazed and enthralled me. Bitten by Jenna's giggle bug, I think my wife and Mamie Rose wished they too would never stop.

After that experience, I vowed never to forget Jenna's lesson in love. Nothing in life was to be taken for granted. Nothing in life was ordinary. Not with my kids. Not unless I let it. Not unless I refuse to enter the Tunnel of Giggles once in awhile.

A Lesson in Compassion

Jenna was shocked as she watched the drama unfold on the ice, where Chris, one of my son's hockey teammates, lay motionless. She often came along with me to her brother's hockey games, mostly to play with a friend, or dance to the music between whistles. If you asked her the score or even the color of her brother's jersey that day, I don't think she knew, or cared. She came only to have fun, her way.

She's seen kids hurt before, but never this way, and never did it affect her. At first, she covered her eyes; she didn't want to see. Then slowly, she picked her head up, and she was no longer ten years old. She was about to learn, too early, what most of us as adults learn painfully—how it hurts to care. For one of the first times in her life, she came face to face with the meaning of compassion. We never expect it to happen this way, but life doesn't send out invitations for such experiences.

The troubling scene on the ice brought out a side of my daughter that tested her character. And my little girl rose triumphantly to the challenge, earning her way into the ranks of a caring humanity. A potentially serious situation showed me a glimpse of her true colors. Jenna was living a wake-up call, one of her first. She, like everyone else in the arena, went from a Disney thrill ride to a sober silence.

Chris wasn't alone on the ice. He was every parent's child, and even my daughter's.

Questions from Jenna came like a torrential downpour, questions I couldn't answer. "What's wrong with him, Daddy? Is it serious? Are they going to take him to the hospital?"

I felt helplessly strange, and thought that when our kids ask small questions, we have all the answers, even if we don't. As the questions become more serious, we become lost for answers. Ever been in this position as a parent? Your kid fires a thousand questions in five seconds, and either you can't or don't know what to answer? All I kept repeating was, "I don't know, Jenna, I don't know."

Then Jenna took my hand, holding it tighter than ever. I could feel her fear; she wasn't alone. Sheepishly she looked at me, and then put her head on my shoulder. I wanted to hide her, to protect her, but it was too late. Someday she'd have to see this for herself. That someday was now. I realized then and there that I couldn't always control or protect my daughter's life. I knew this would happen, but not this early and certainly not this way.

Suddenly, everyone was cheering, as Chris started to move. Minutes later, he got up, with the help of his father and coach. The applause grew louder, becoming almost deafening with each slow step he took. But it was strange too; almost as soon as Chris made his way to the bench, parents went back to shouting and cheering for their sides. It was back to us against them. "Let's play hockey," yelled the referee....

Chris soon was back on the ice and played great. My son's team won, 4-3, scoring the last goal with five seconds left, with Chris getting an assist. As usual with victory, the whole team ran onto the ice and jumped on the goalie, congratulating him. Chris's brush with injury seemed already forgotten, lost in the sweetness of victory.

I turned to my daughter. Before I could utter a word, she asked, "Does his head still hurt, Daddy? Don't you think he should go to the doctor? Are you sure he'll be okay, Daddy?"

"Honestly, Jenna, I don't know, but I hope so. But I do know who will be okay."

"Who, Daddy?" she asked.

"You, Jenna," I answered.

"Why will I be okay, Daddy?"

"Because, unlike others here, you didn't forget, you didn't go right back to the game. You learned your lesson here. And you're only ten years old."

"What about the parents, Daddy? They care, don't they?"

"Of course they do," I said.

"It's just a game, Daddy, right?"

"Yes, Jenna," I said. "It's just a game."

As we walked out of the arena, watching the parents from both sides, I wondered if it was only a ten-year-old who understood that.

The Man of the House

Although my wife's four-day business trip was still a week away, I was already going into withdrawal. Laure was leaving me on my own with two kids and a brand new puppy, in a house we'd moved into just two weeks earlier.

There were more boxes piled up than in a Circuit City warehouse. Sasha, the puppy, wasted no time leaving her trademark all over the house. And my kids, who'd promised and promised they'd take care of the dog, somehow suffered from a sudden bout of amnesia.

My trying to convince my wife to postpone her trip fell on deaf ears. "I planned this a long time ago," she said. "I can't change it now." Then, as she left, seeing me practically on my knees, she added, "Well, at least you won't be bored."

Oh, she was right. I wasn't going to be bored. I may not be alive when she gets back, or may be in an insane asylum, but I certainly wasn't going to be bored. We agreed on that completely.

I was expecting a Thursday to Sunday from hell. What I got was a four-day roller coaster ride that made me realize how many thrills I was missing. As a father, I tended to do what I think most dads did, play the absentee landlords on the day-to-day routine of running a home. The next four days would make all that come to a screeching halt.

It began before dawn on Thursday, just minutes after Laure left for the airport. Downstairs, Sasha was alternating between wailing and barking. "What did I get myself into?" I thought. Like most of the normal world, my kids were fast asleep.

The realization at 5:30 a.m. that I'd soon have to make my kids' lunches didn't exactly add to my comfort level. What was I going to make for them? "Maybe I'll get lucky," I thought, "and Laure's company will cancel her trip at the last minute and send her home."

Of course, I didn't get lucky, but somehow we survived the first morning. "Great!" I thought, "Only three-and-half days to go."

By 5:00 p.m., Jeremy and Jenna would be home from school, so I had to make sure I was there and getting supper ready. I'd promised Laure I wouldn't order any take-out meals, at least until Saturday. I have to admit it was one of the most difficult promises I ever had to keep.

By Friday night, I was in shock. Did my wife do all this and work full time too? I was always there for the "big stuff," I thought, the nights and weekends. But this stuff, this day-by-day ritual the family went through, I realized I wasn't part of. I was a stranger, sitting on the outside, watching.

By Saturday morning, I'd foolishly talked myself into thinking I was now on top of my game. I'd become the new master. I was in control—control of nothing, I was soon to discover. After taking Sasha for her early walk, and stopping at the bakery for some bread, I realized I'd lost my keys and would have to wake the kids to get back in.

It was now 6:30. Jenna, eleven, and Jeremy, thirteen, liked to sleep in. Needless to say, they weren't happy with me for waking them up. Given the fact that it took me almost half-an-hour to rouse them didn't exactly boost my spirits either, especially in light of some unwanted attention I'd attracted.

After I'd been ringing the doorbell for about fifteen minutes, a police cruiser going by stopped, and the officer came up and asked me for identification. Naturally, I'd left my wallet in the house. When my kids finally came to the door, let's just say it wasn't exactly a happy reunion of father and children.

That night, when Laure called and asked how things were going, the kids naturally went into every embarrassing detail. Sometimes I think kids are natural born reporters. They call it exactly the way they see it and never leave out any of the details.

When Laure came home Sunday night, I was happy to see her, but a little sad that my short-lived stint at being mom and dad had come to an end. By not being there, she gave me an opportunity to get a glimpse into the real life of our family, the cement that kept our bricks together.

I always believed if I was part of the big things, I was doing okay—the trips, the dinners out, and going to the kids' ball games. Nothing could be further from the truth, I learned. Whether my wife intended it or not, she'd let me in on a glorious little secret by going away for a few days. The so-called everyday, small, year-in and year-out things a family did were the real things—making the kids' lunches and helping them with their homework, for example.

Those things lasted much longer in their hearts than any fancy dinner at a restaurant or taking them to a hockey game. I learned that it's the little things the kids remember most. Somehow, the hugs always seemed tighter, longer, and stronger after an hour helping with homework or just sharing our day, than if we'd had a big night on the town.

A Little Corner of Heaven

L eave it to my ten-year-old daughter Jenna to take me on a personal tour of the human heart. After months of feeling low, following the collapse of my business and going to work for someone else, I finally found the courage to ask Jenna to be the first one in my family to see my tiny new office. She had a day off from school with nowhere to go, and was still too young to be left alone.

At work, I was still feeling very much like a stranger in a strange land but, from the moment Jenna entered the building, my world changed. One by one, my co-workers were captivated by her and started to engage her in conversation. Suddenly, as if by magic, concerns about business vanished. Instead of talking about the latest sales figures, everyone began exchanging their favorite stories about their kids. Pictures began popping out of wallets, as financial reports changed to family reports.

I was amazed! What was it about Jenna that brought this out in everyone? What is it about all kids that brings this out in adults? Then, my thoughts were interrupted when my friend Mitchell came in and asked Jenna if she'd like to see pictures of his kids. She, of course, said "Yes," and proceeded to follow him down the hall to his office.

Two minutes later, I heard a shriek. It was Jenna. I ran to find out what was going on. "Look, Daddy, look," she said. "Do you believe it? Look at all these pictures of his kids. They're beautiful!"

I just smiled. Mitchell was beyond smiling, his face glowing with happiness at Jenna's words: "Looks like heaven, Daddy, don't you think?"

"That's a good way of putting it, Jenna. It's Mitchell's little corner of heaven."

In typical ten-year-old fashion, Jenna was now ready for the next adventure. "Let's go visit other offices, Daddy," she said.

"But everyone's working, Jenna. It's a bad time."

"Maybe it's the best time," suggested Mitchell. "How often does your daughter come? Besides, whenever anyone's kids come, everything stops and we all pull out the memories."

I wasn't sure if we were doing the right thing or not but at this point there was no stopping us.

Pictures, pictures, and more pictures of kids dominated the office landscape. Everyone had an office, some big, some small. But none of this mattered when it came to pictures of their kids. Office sizes became irrelevant. The real treasures, the really priceless works of art, were the same for all.

Children were everywhere, in every scene you could imagine, in every smile you could smile, and in every face you could see. These pictures represented the dreams of their lives. Pictures of kids outnumbered all others, with pets coming a distant second, and husbands and wives a hidden third.

"It's amazing, Daddy, isn't it?" said Jenna. "This is a big place and everyone here has a little corner of heaven."

"It is amazing, Jenna," I agreed, not sure which of us was more amazed. But it didn't matter.

By then, it was getting close to lunchtime and I told Jenna we needed to let everyone get back to work. But as we walked back to my office, I could feel something was different. I began seeing my colleagues in a new light. It was as if I had just walked with Alice through the looking glass into a different world from the one I had known just a few minutes earlier.

Then, as I looked at Jenna waiting for me to get ready to take her to lunch, I realized I had entered another world—the little corner of

72

heaven that was there all the time. I knew it, but before today I had looked only with my eyes. Jenna showed me how blind I was. What my little girl taught me that day was that in order to see what really matters in life, we must look with our hearts and not merely with our eyes.

I Love a Messy House!

It was a happy day. My son Jeremy was back from summer camp. When I saw him step off the bus, I couldn't believe my eyes. This couldn't possibly be the little boy I'd last seen two months earlier. Wasn't it only yesterday that my wife Laure and I sent him off on his first summer adventure?

I remembered it so well. Jeremy couldn't wait to get on the bus, but I couldn't stop saying goodbye. He made sure whatever hugs and kisses we got from him were not within sight of his friends. Heaven forbid!

Now he was back, looking so mature. There have been few times in my life when I've been so happy to see someone. As soon as he spotted me, he ran over and hugged and kissed me—right in front of his friends and their parents. True, all the kids were doing the same, but that didn't matter. This was a first, one I'd never forget. Despite the mob around us, I didn't hear or see anyone but Jeremy.

He started talking about his summer, and couldn't stop. "My counselor wants to meet you, Dad, and then we have to go around to the other side to get my bags."

"OK, then what do you want to do, Jeremy?" I asked.

"Go to McDonald's, of course."

"Of course," I said. "And then?"

"Then I just want to go home and take an hour-long hot shower."

After we ate, I dropped him off at our house, while I ran an errand. When I returned, a few minutes later, I could hardly believe my eyes. The house was a disaster, the full extent of which became clear as I made my way into each room. It looked like a hurricane had blown through, wreaking havoc everywhere!

No room had been spared. All sorts of sports equipment had been thrown wildly about. Half a Big Mac was lying cold on the kitchen table, the other half in the den, next to our TV. And the bathroom! Oh, the bathroom! It was straight out of a college fraternity house movie—close to unbearable.

I thought, "Is this what I brought my son up for? So that one day he'd have a hurricane named in his honor?" But who was I fooling? I loved it! No, I didn't. I kept arguing with myself. How could I love a hurricane?

Then I realized if there was ever such a thing as a Kid Forgiveness Day, today would be it. Jeremy could do practically anything today and, because I'd missed him so much, I'd keep looking the other way. I wonder if kids know that about their parents—that there may be a day now and then when they can say or do almost anything, with a good chance of getting away with it.

Thousands of times, mostly every day, I'd tell Jeremy to clean up this, throw away that, turn off the lights, etc., etc., etc. He somehow seemed to forget he didn't have an army of butlers at his beck and call. And even if he did, it would have taken them weeks to clean up what looked like a towel factory gone berserk.

Funny how when we're young we promise ourselves we'd be nothing like our parents. Yet when we become parents, we find so many of their traits have crept into our own lives—like it or not.

For years, my mother badgered me about keeping our house spic-and-span. For years, I either ignored her or locked my door. Now I find myself behaving the same way to my kids. Don't do this. Don't do that. Pick up this. Pick up that. If I ever took time to listen to myself, maybe I'd have heard how I sounded, but I never bothered.

I'd never let up and couldn't understand why it took him so long to get it. Maybe, I thought, giving him the benefit of the doubt, it was just because he was a boy of thirteen, and that it came with the territory. But "no," I declared, right is right, and constantly leaving messes wherever he went was *not* right!

But not having my son around for two long months changed my perspective, at least for the moment. So, when I walked straight into Hurricane Jeremy, the mess didn't matter. Having my son back was what mattered. A clean house didn't seem quite so important. I reminded myself that Jeremy's heart was never a mess; he never needed to be reminded to clean it up. *That's* what was important. And I had to remember it—not just today, when it was easy, but tomorrow and the next day, and next year, when it could be hard.

Chairlift to the Stars

In my experience, there's no better sport for the whole family than downhill skiing. It can bring out the best in families—eventually!

During a recent brief winter vacation, we went to a ski resort called Mont Blanc. The weather was perfect and so was the hill. But we hadn't been skiing for more than a year, and it showed.

Skiing can be a battle, make no mistake about that. As with every great victory, you don't get to celebrate without a struggle. And struggle you do. One boring, aggravating routine follows another, especially when it comes to putting on ski boots.

Ah! The infamous ski boots. Who in the world invented ski boots? Whoever it was, I don't think they've ever even seen a kid. By the time I put my kids' boots on, I'm ready for a nap. It then takes me almost ten minutes to put on my own boots, which I hate doing. Where's Michael J. Fox when you need him? In *Back to the Future III*, he puts on skateboard boots that automatically adjust to his feet. He doesn't move a muscle. Now that's my kind of boot.

Finally, we're ready—it's time to ski! As usual, for the first couple of runs, we all skied together. As usual, my son complained that we were slowing him down. Jeremy was the daredevil in the family. And few things scare parents more than kids who have no fear. No fear is

79

dangerous and gets people into trouble. Half the time, I'm yelling at Jeremy to slow down and watch the trees.

After a few runs, followed by a lunch break, we were ready for more. By then, it was after 2:00 p.m. and the sun was already starting to set. As everyone knows, a winter day without the sun feels fifteen to twenty degrees colder and, with the wind atop the mountains, it can become brutal as the day wears on.

We decided to split up, with my wife Laure going off with Jeremy, while Jenna and I skied together. "We'll meet at 3:30 at the ticket booth," Laure shouted back as she and my son got on the chairlift.

"Hurry up, Daddy, we don't have much time," Jenna reminded me. "Okay, okay, Jenna, I'm coming."

Seconds after we boarded the chairlift, the magic began. Now I knew why it was worth all the hassle. Now I knew why skiing was such a great family sport. Like every sport, there was a struggle. Then, if you persevere, victory comes. And best of all, savoring the victory!

With Jenna and me alone on that chairlift, she started chattering away. Words spilled from her mouth. "Imagine if this chairlift had a CD player, Daddy, or a place to warm your hands."

I tried to tell her that wasn't the point of it all, that there was enough of all that "techie" stuff all around us everywhere we went, every minute of every day. That it was nice to find someplace where we could escape it all, with our voices and the whispering wind in the trees making the only sounds.

I tried to tell her all this, but her next suggestion stopped me and left me speechless. "Imagine, Daddy, that this chairlift would never stop!"

"What do you mean, Jenna?" I was baffled by her comment. "Imagine that it would take us all the way to the stars?"

At this point, we were near the top, and it was time to get off. I concentrated so much on us jumping off properly, that I didn't have a chance to answer her.

Then, standing there on that mountaintop with my precious young daughter, I realized all the hassles of getting ready were worth it. The battles were over, and it was time to celebrate our victory. And by the way, I never did get to tell Jenna, but that chairlift did indeed take us to the stars—and dropped us somewhere along the Milky Way.

My SNAPSHOT of HEAVEN

WRITE YOUR OWN EVERYDAY MOMENT

My SNAPSHOT
of HEAVEN

Section Two:
Special Occasions

*"Love doesn't make the world go round.
Love is what makes the ride worthwhile."*

Franklin P. Jones (1853-1935)

Ruby Slippers

We waited all year until Easter rolled around and *The Wizard of Oz* was played on TV. It was 1961. I was eight years old. There were no videos, no DVDs, no 500 channels. It was a big deal in our neighborhood. Everyone would gather at our house to watch this little girl named Dorothy from Kansas swept up by a tornado, ending up in some mythical magic land called Oz.

Every year, we sat awe-struck in front of the TV, as Dorothy had to defeat the Wicked Witch of the West to get to see the all-powerful Wizard, who they said could grant you any wish your heart desired.

What always confused my friends and me was why would Dorothy want to go home? To us, the few minutes we saw of this faraway place called Kansas couldn't compare to Oz. It had everything Kansas didn't have. Especially for a kid of eight, it was hard to understand why Dorothy was so unhappy. I never understood or cared to understand the whole point of this beautiful story, until years later.

Before my son Jeremy and my daughter Jenna could talk, I made sure the tradition continued. Easter was Dorothy's day in our house. For several hours, the future, and even the present, was on hold. It was great. When it came to the end I cried. I couldn't help it. I always cried at the end of *The Wizard of Oz*. At first, when my kids were very young,

I had to go out of the room and cry, because they'd think something was wrong and start to cry too.

"Shhhh, everyone," I'd warn, as the movie began. "Here it comes."

Suddenly, our home wasn't our home. We were in Oz, with Dorothy. Great movies do that, I realized. They take you along for the ride. And what a ride this was, as the beautiful Good Witch told Dorothy the startling news. It was so simple, so utterly, completely, ridiculously simple. All along on her feet were the ruby slippers, her ticket home. As a parent, something that always bugged me, hit me even harder at this moment. How come, I thought, even when the credits roll, so many of us forget this? We forget the ruby slippers.

The next year, I was away on a business trip, halfway around the world. Unfortunately, I was going to miss watching *The Wizard of Oz* with my kids. This was the first time I was ever away so long and so far. I wasn't happy, but had no choice. I'd been depressed for days leading up to the big event, so I made sure I timed myself to call home (there was a twelve-hour time difference) at the precise moment Dorothy found out about the ruby slippers.

As I called the operator to place the overseas call, my eyes started to get a little watery. I spoke first with my son Jeremy, and then my wife. I told them how much I missed them and how lonely I was. They reminded me that I'd be home before I knew it. Then Jenna took the phone. I don't know why, but I always seemed to speak to her last.

She listened to me repeat myself. Then, she stopped me cold in my tracks. "Daddy, like you always said, remember the ruby slippers and you'll feel better." I couldn't believe my ears.

"What's that you said, Jenna?" I heard her perfectly the first time, but just wanted to hear her say it again.

"Remember the ruby slippers, Daddy. Do what Dorothy did. Click three times and you'll be home."

All I could say to Jenna was, "I love you, and I have to hang up now."

There was something I knew I had to do, but first I looked out the window, in the closets, and underneath the bed. Only then, and only then, did I click three times.

I must have seen *The Wizard of Oz* more than a thousand times. After hanging up from talking with Jenna, I realized I'd never before gotten the message. It could never be the Wizard; he wasn't real. Only the real things in life make you happy. Only the real things in life show you the way home. Our kids are the real magic in our lives. The rest are just wizards.

Love Letters 101

Ever wait for something your whole life, unaware you were waiting for it until you found it? That's exactly what happened to me when, on my thirty-sixth birthday, I received my first love letter—my first real love letter. My son Jeremy had just turned six and finally was learning how to write. He was so proud of himself.

It was just in time to write his father a homemade birthday card. No disrespect to Hallmark, but homemade is homemade, especially when it comes hand delivered from your son.

"Sit on the couch, Daddy," Jeremy ordered. "Just sit and listen." These were orders I could take for the rest of my life, and never complain.

"Are you ready, Daddy?" he asked, with a smile so wide you felt like you were caught in this web of joy and hoped never to get free. "Ready," I repeated to Jeremy.

Ready? I've been ready my whole life. The floor was his. The world stood still—at least my world. The phone rang; I ignored it. Then the doorbell rang; I ignored it, too. "Go on, Jeremy," I urged. "Read, read!" And read he did.

In just four lines, he changed my life. In just four lines, he taught me something I never knew before. And then he sealed it with a great big hug and kiss and said, "This is for you, Daddy!"

He never understood how right he was. This was for me, and only me—my little forever love letter that will never be played on a radio station, never be seen in a movie theater, and certainly never found in any bookstore.

As Jeremy handed me his card, saying those magic words: "This is yours, Daddy," he cast a spell on me that will never go away. Ever since that day, I've understood what real love letters are—the kind that could only have been written by a son or a daughter. Jeremy's words would never make the cover of *TIME*, or the headlines on CNN, but who cared? They made it into my heart, and made my life worth living.

As the years passed, Jeremy's birthday letters got better and better. But it wasn't just his words that became clear and more sophisticated, it was the way he said them. He obviously had a gift for words and was able to string them together in innovative ways. Soon, he added music. One year he was Billy Joel, and sang "The Piano Man" tune, with his own words. Another year Jeremy and his sister Jenna did a duet to the hit songs of *Grease*.

Every year brought a surprise. I never believed my birthdays could be so good. And as the years passed, my library of cards grew and grew. It was clear over the passage of time how adult-like Jeremy's words and pictures became. Eventually, by the time he was about nine or ten, he dropped the pictures.

Isn't that like what we adults do? Somehow, pictures are another piece of our childhood that we think silly and no longer relevant in our lives, until of course we hit a certain age when the clocks in our minds start to slow and we yearn for yesterday.

So as we age and become so-called "wise," we drop pieces of our childhood along our way like litter, only to one day wish we hadn't.

Jeremy insisted on writing his own birthday cards for me. He wasn't interested in buying cards. They didn't say what *he* wanted to say. Eventually my wallet become so fat, not because of money or credit cards, but because of Jeremy's letters, that I had to get a second wallet just for them.

I always carry his letters with me, to remind me what really matters, and to make me smile, especially when smiling is the last thing in the world I want to do.

When Jeremy was six, I'd enrolled in his class, Love Letters 101. I learned a long time ago that to do anything well in life, it takes years of practice and devotion to graduate. On my fiftieth birthday, Jeremy did just that. He wrote me a card that had me in tears and, as a bonus, maybe to say, "You graduated with honors, Pops," he did something he'd never done before.

He came over and hugged me for about five minutes—five minutes that seemed to last an eternity. And who can say it didn't?

What a Weekend!

From the day my son Jeremy was born, I dreamed of him growing up and playing sports with me, like he was one of my friends. Maybe it's just a guy thing. But I envisioned him pitching a baseball so fast that it felt like a hole was being burned in my glove. Or shooting a slap shot that felt like a sharp wind over my head as the puck hit the upper corner of the net.

As my baby son became a little boy, my dream began coming true. Whatever sports we played, I felt I was playing with my best friend. It was great. But I was saving my biggest sports surprise for him as he approached his tenth birthday. Even my wife was caught off guard. After all, a double-digit birthday is a very special one, and this called for a very special celebration.

Hockey had always been Jeremy's favorite sport. Coincidentally, his birthday fell on the same weekend when he was playing in two hockey games near our home and the Montreal Canadiens were playing their only game of the year in Toronto. We'd never been to the Toronto Maple Leafs Arena, the Air Canada Center, or to Toronto's famed Hockey Hall of Fame. The timing was perfect, and we weren't going to miss the opportunity. It was to be our weekend of a lifetime.

A month before the big day came, I started making the arrangements. I left nothing to chance. Everything had to be timed to the min-

97

ute, since we were packing into forty-eight hours events that would normally take a week. The days leading up to our big weekend were filled with intense anticipation for both of us. I don't know who was more excited or nervous. Maybe Jeremy was more excited, but I definitely was more nervous.

For days we talked nothing but hockey, hockey, hockey. Then, at last, the famous weekend came.

Jeremy's first game was at 2:00 p.m. in Montreal, and our plane to Toronto was scheduled to leave at 4:15. During his game, I must have looked at my watch a thousand times. Naturally his game started late and was a nail biter right to the end, when my son broke a 2-2 tie in the dying seconds to win it for his team. The arena erupted in applause. I lived for these moments. My wife often asks me why I go to all of Jeremy's games and practices. My answer is always the same, because someday I won't be able to.

I tried ignoring the excitement around us as I ushered Jeremy into the dressing room. In record speed, we made it to the airport and were at the gate ready to go, without a minute to spare. There was just enough time to catch our breath. Then almost before we knew it, we were touching down at Toronto's Pearson Airport.

I had arranged another surprise for Jeremy—a limousine, filled with all kinds of hockey memorabilia.

At 6:30 sharp, just thirty minutes before game time, we made our grand entrance at the Air Canada Center. Our seats were great. My son and I weren't just in another city; we were in another time and place. At this point, I could have kept going, arena to arena, never coming back, just Jeremy and me. This was the first evening of our fairy tale—a parent's story I'd remember forever.

Unfortunately, however, the game was very forgettable—nothing short of a disaster for the Canadiens. Finally the nightmare was over. We were both exhausted and couldn't wait to get to our hotel and hit the pillows.

The next morning, we arrived at the Hockey Hall of Fame just as it opened. Each room was filled with hockey history. I watched Jeremy's eyes turn around and around as he tried to take in more than he could absorb. A hundred years of hockey triumphs and disasters waited for us in each room. We didn't know where to look first.

Each exhibit, each video, each locker room was more amazing than the other. In these rooms everyone became ten years old. Everyone remembered playing with their friends or maybe their fathers on the local ice. As we rounded the last corner, there it stood, the crowning jewel, the stuff they say dreams are made of—the Stanley Cup.

We both just stared. Not saying a word to each other. I reached for his hand. He first looked around and then took mine.

But, like all fairy tales, I had to break the spell. One look at my watch and I knew we had to go. Just in time, we boarded the plane back to Montreal and made his second game two minutes into the first period.

When we got home later, Jeremy talked a mile a minute, telling his mother every detail of our hockey weekend. "Do you think, Daddy, that Wayne Gretsky ever had such a weekend?" he asked.

"I doubt it, Jeremy. I doubt it." He then went upstairs to wash up for dinner. When a half-hour went by and he didn't come back down, I went to look for him.

There was my hockey champ, still fully dressed, fast asleep on his bed. All I could think of was the smile the sight would bring to his hockey idol, Wayne Gretsky. I think even Gretsky would have agreed that what made my heart dance wasn't the young hockey star fast asleep. No, it was the little boy with whom this dad was so lucky to have shared a weekend to remember.

The Doll Castle in the Sky

I t's never been easy finding something to do with my daughter. Because of my passion for sports, I tend to focus on activities that are more fun for Jeremy than for Jenna. So I've always had to work harder at finding things to do with her.

After weeks of scouring the newspapers for ideas, I finally hit the jackpot. I raced into Jenna's bedroom to tell her the news. "Jenna, in two weeks, there's going to be a large antique doll exhibition dating back over a hundred years. It'll be held on top of the Olympic Tower, about thirty stories in the air." She jumped out of her seat and raced over to give me a hug.

The great day finally arrived. Jenna had been talking about it all week and I think everybody in town knew we were going on this great adventure in the sky. "I can hardly wait, Daddy," she said, as we were on our way. "Now, what are we going to see? Are there really dolls from one hundred years ago? What kind of dolls did little girls like me play with then, Daddy? What did they do all day if they didn't have TVs or video games or movies?" She kept firing away with questions as I drove.

"Let's go, Jenna," I said, as I parked the car. After picking up our tickets, we got on the large elevator that would take us to the sky. We

101

closed our eyes for a moment, and it felt like we were going through the clouds, toward our final destination.

Before we even stepped off the elevator, the dream got into full swing. A lady wearing clothes from the 1800s greeted us, along with two little girls dressed the same way, holding dolls from that era. It was like we'd entered a time tunnel. No words could describe the look on my daughter's face—her eyes glued almost magically to the sight. She turned to me and her smile spoke of the beauty of the evening that had only just begun.

We walked around, admiring the different exhibitions. I held her hand as we talked about what little girls were doing 150 years ago. I realized this was one of those peaks—those magical, fleeting moments you can never get a handle on.

Each showcase was detailed and made you a doll lover in no time, no matter how little you cared about dolls when you'd arrived. The parade of parents with their daughters was a sight in itself. Expressions of incredible joy and surprise and genuine curiosity seemed to cover each little girl's face. They asked hundreds of questions and couldn't take their eyes off the immensity of the show. I wondered what the real show was: the doll exhibitions or the children's reactions to them.

No doll show would be complete without the most famous doll of all—Barbie. We learned, in great detail, how Barbie evolved. I quickly realized how much Barbie was a reflection of her times, as her clothes and friends changed over the years.

Like most girls her age, Jenna was a Barbie nut. She was obsessed with the Barbie car, the Barbie boat, the Barbie house, and all the clothes and accessories that went with them. Jenna was especially fascinated by the Barbie of the '60s. She was even more amazed by her accessories, especially the television and record player.

"Look at that funny-looking toaster!" she said. "Why did they wear so many hats? Boy, did they love pink, Pops."

The last and most exciting exhibition was an interactive one. Inside a gigantic glass cage was a huge globe of the world, covered with miniature dolls dressed in their country's native costume. Outside the case were buttons that made each doll and her country light up. Jenna pushed each button with complete innocence and disbelief.

By then, it was late and we were both getting tired. I asked Jenna for a little kiss on my cheek and suggested it was time to go. I told her it was close to midnight and, like Cinderella, soon the magic would end. She just looked at me and laughed.

We got home just past midnight. I carried my sleeping Cinderella up to her bed, tucked her in, and probably kissed her a hundred times. Before I left her room, I thanked her for an unforgettable night, knowing she was asleep and couldn't hear me. Then, just as I was halfway out her door, she said in a muffled, quiet voice, "You're welcome, Daddy. Thanks! I love you, too."

I just smiled and left her room. Glancing at my watch, I saw it was after midnight, way past Cinderella time. In the fairy tale, Cinderella turns back from a princess into an ordinary maid at midnight. But that's just in a fairy tale. The real Cinderella was sleeping peacefully in the next room, and she will always be my princess, no matter what the hour.

The Truck of Dreams

I t was only a rental pickup truck. As white as snow, and every time you jumped on the back you felt like you were in a John Wayne movie, speeding across your thousand-acre cattle ranch deep in the heart of Texas. It was only a week, during a visit to our in-laws in Naples, Florida, but that pickup became the highlight of our trip. Every time my kids climbed aboard, they smiled from ear to ear, looking like they were ready for some big adventure.

"This truck is so cool, Pops," said my son Jeremy.

"I love the color, Daddy," said my daughter Jenna. They were both comfortably perched in back.

"C'mon," I called, "one of you sit up front with me."

"No, no," they shouted in chorus. "We love it back here."

I couldn't believe it and never expected it, but that white truck was the star of the week. To my kids, it was like a big toy that moved fast. As we drove around, I could see them beaming. Wherever we went, no matter how close it was, they refused to walk. They had to ride in the pickup. Before the week was half over, my wife must have taken more than twenty-five pictures with my kids in different poses—all in back of that truck.

Everything went into the truck—towels, bathing suits, sandals, and even things the kids didn't need. They kept piling in the stuff, telling me over and over again: "Daddy, it is a truck, right?"

"Yes," I kept saying, "but not that kind of truck."

This year the weather couldn't have been better. It was hot and clear almost every day. The beaches were great and we played tennis once a day. But none of this mattered. All my kids kept talking about was the white pickup truck. At one point, Jenna remarked, "It's not a truck, Daddy. Let's pretend it's something else. It's soooo cool."

"What should it be? Jenna," I asked.

"Let's play a game, Daddy."

"A game, Jenna? With the truck?"

"Yes," she continued.

"What kind of game?" I knew Jenna had a great imagination, but a game in a pickup truck? I couldn't imagine what she had in mind.

"Pretend, just pretend, Daddy, that we're on a safari."

"A safari? Where did you learn about safaris?" I asked.

"On TV, of course. Well anyway, pretend we're on a safari, just you, me and Jeremy, something like *Jurassic Park*, and we're all in this white truck looking for the dinosaurs—except there's one problem."

"Which is?" I asked, not having a clue what was coming.

"Well, dinosaurs hate white," she explained. "It's like bulls hate red, Daddy."

At this point, I was more caught off guard by her knowledge than her story. "Jenna, where do you learn all this?"

"TV, of course," she said.

"Of course," I replied.

"So remember, Daddy. We're dodging these huge dinosaurs, right and left. They breathe fire, knock down trees, and throw big rocks at us, just missing the truck. Jeremy and I are in the back, yelling and screaming all the way. What do you think, Daddy? Good story?"

"The story's great, Jenna, great! Where did you get such an imagination?"

"I'm a kid, Daddy. You know that. We all have a great imagination. Don't adults have a great imagination?"

"Not really," I said. "Most of us lose it when we get older. We're too busy."

"Too busy! At what, Daddy?"

I wasn't sure what to say. "Just too busy, having kids, working, that sort of thing."

"Is that good, Daddy?" she asked. She was serious. And for a moment so was I. But I never answered her question. Not because of her, but because of me. I didn't want to hear what I was going to say.

Three days later, it was time to go home. I dropped the family off at the terminal with all the bags, and went to take the white truck back to the rental place. Usually, I go alone. This time, however, both Jenna and Jeremy wanted to come with me. Or, should I say, they wanted one more ride in their chariot. We all loved that truck.

As I drove into the rental return area and gave back the keys, we all said good-bye to our snow-white truck, the truck of dreams that had brought us safely back from our dangerous encounter with those fire-breathing, rock-throwing dinosaurs in far off Africa.

The Pride of the Yankees

W e never knew it was coming, our suppertime interrupted by the great baseball hero, Joe DiMaggio, the pride of the Yankees. At least that's what my son Jeremy looked like to us, decked out in full uniform, announcing that he'd just made the local baseball team, the Mount Royal Yankees.

In minutes, our kitchen was transported to the Bronx, and became the Yankee locker room. What a sight that I wasn't prepared for. Even my daughter Jenna, who usually doesn't get too excited about her brother's sport endeavors, looked in amazement at him wearing his Yankees baseball uniform. The famous pinstripe uniform always looked great on Babe Ruth, Lou Gehrig, and Yogi Berra. But on my son Jeremy, it was magical, almost as if it came to life—a perfect copy of the real thing.

"So, slugger, what position did you make?" I asked.

"Center field, Pops. Can you believe it, Pops, me in center field?" He was so excited. And seeing him so happy started to get me excited too, right then and there. No sight on earth could have equaled the thrill of seeing my son in his baseball uniform. Of all the sports uniforms, none were more made for each other than that of baseball pinstripes and a young boy.

Jeremy was so proud of himself, and rightly so. Though he had made the baseball team two years ago, this time was much more significant. Last time he only played half the season, after being hit in the eye with a baseball. That whole scene had been pretty scary at first, but Jeremy came through okay. He'd rejoined the team in the playoffs, but I could see he wasn't the same. Last year, he decided to pass. He didn't even try out.

So, when he walked in, this young Joe DiMaggio, beaming from ear to ear, the house went into an uproar. Our imaginations started to take hold. It was the bottom of the ninth, two outs, bases loaded, DiMaggio up. The count is three and two. Then, bang! DiMaggio hits it out of Ebbets Field, beating those pesky Brooklyn Dodgers and winning the World Series. The place goes wild and so did our kitchen.

"So, you want to play catch, Pops?"

"But I'm..." Then I stopped myself. I hadn't finished eating, but who cared? I wouldn't always have this moment. Jeremy wanted only me and I could feel it. He wanted to be with his father, and I wanted to be with my son. "Sure, Jeremy, let's go." No more words were necessary. Laure understood completely.

"Where are we going, Pops?"

"Well, since you're wearing a real baseball uniform and a Yankee one, we have to go the real diamond in the center of town."

Jeremy looked at me, paused, and then just smiled. It was the kind of smile that told me he was thinking the same thing. But he wanted the words to come from me.

"Good idea, Daddyo, let's go."

An hour later, it started to get dark, and the lights came on. More and more, this was looking like the real thing. It was just past 9:00 p.m. "Still want to play, Jeremy?"

"Sure, why not. I'm having a lot of fun, Pops."

"Me too, Jeremy."

That summer night in July was perfect baseball weather. We lost track of time; just two guys of summer, playing as if there never would be a tomorrow. The hours flew by. We took turns playing all the greats, Ty Cobb, Roger Maris, and, of course, the infamous Shoeless Joe Jackson. For some reason, he was Jeremy's favorite. It was probably because he was in Jeremy's favorite sport movie, *Field of Dreams*.

"Do you think it's really possible, Daddy?" asked Jeremy.

110

"What?" I yelled back from home plate.

"You know, Pops, what happened in *Field of Dreams*, all those famous players coming out of the fields playing baseball in the middle of...where was it, Pops?"

"Iowa," I answered.

"Well, what do you think, Pops?" He kept on talking. "But I guess it's just a movie. Things like that don't happen in real life. Miracles don't really happen, right, Daddy?"

I just looked up and then at my son—I knew they did.

By the way, if you ever get to the Baseball Hall of Fame in Cooperstown, New York, be sure to look us up. We were inducted that night. Jeremy and I are in the invisible father and son exhibit at the end of the first floor. You won't see us unless you take a kid with you.

He'll find us. Get him to read you the plaque under our exhibit:

"Inducted July 2002, one of the greatest baseball teams ever to set foot on a diamond – Father and Son."

My Girl – Forever!

J enna and I had five minutes to kill before her school bus arrived. I was on my cell phone, checking for messages. Jenna was telling me what her day was going to be like, but I'm not sure I heard what she said.

I had one message, and asked Jenna to look through my glove compartment for a pen, so I could write down a number. It seemed to take her forever. Finally she pulls out a dusty audiocassette and asks if it's from "my time." I love those "my time" questions from my kids. Somehow "my time," coming from her or my son sounds like I went out for supper with Napoleon.

"Let me see it, Jenna, and I'll tell you if it's from *my time*." Sure enough, it was an old tape from the '60s.

"Why didn't you show it to me before, Daddy?"

"I never thought about, I guess. I never thought you'd like it."

"Why not?" She bluntly asked. Indeed, I said to myself, why not? Why wouldn't my ten-year-old daughter like The Temptations? They're fun, great to dance to, and even more fun to sing along with. Who said there were rules? Who said some things aren't gold forever? Songs of the heart are forever.

As these thoughts began racing through my mind, I started to feel like a kid again. "Do you want to hear it, Jenna?"

"Of course, but hurry up, Daddy. The bus will be here any minute." Five seconds later, "My Girl" started to play. Fireworks! Magic! No longer were we sitting in the car waiting for a school bus. It felt like the world had stopped. No buses. No deadlines. No school. No appointments. And no phone calls.

As The Temptations hit their chorus, a smile the size of the universe covered Jenna's face. It was a look that cast a thousand rainbows in the sky. A look that made you feel your car had just blasted off like a rocket ship past the Milky Way, on its way to the moon. It was a look you carried in your heart wherever you went, like a treasured photo in a wallet.

Suddenly, Jenna began to snap her fingers and tap her feet to the intoxicating beat. Though she'd never heard the song before, as The Temptations began to repeat their chorus, she joined in, "I know you say, what can make me feel this way, My Girl, My Girl."

At this point I had no choice; I had to join my daughter. Within seconds both of us were shouting the chorus at the top of our lungs. We replayed it several times, until the bus arrived. From then on, Jenna wanted only me to take her to the school bus. I felt the same way. With The Temptations waiting for you, who could resist?

The next day we really got into full swing. We purposely started to get to the bus stop earlier, so we could sing the entire song together. This soon became the highlight of my day—it was unbelievable. What seemed to start out merely as an audition had somehow become a command performance at Carnegie Hall.

With the car windows down, and the music blasting at 8:00 on a weekday morning, I felt totally out of sync with the rest of the world. While they were hurrying by on their way to work, we were making a brief stop at the Hollywood Bowl, rocking with The Temptations.

Each day I looked forward to those moments with Jenna, more and more. No matter what problems I had to face, I knew the morning concert with Jenna would help ease me through. But I never realized how precious, how irreplaceable, those moments were until I took a recent business trip.

On my way to an appointment, "My Girl" came blasting through the radio like magic. It was the first time in months I heard the song without Jenna. It was still great, but not the same. There was no magic. Something, or rather someone, was missing.

114

I realized it wasn't the song, it was never the song. It was singing with Jenna that was magic—Jenna and The Temptations! It was my moment in the sun. She made the trip to the Milky Way and to the moon possible.

I realized my heart had become a library, storing up forever memories of my kids, the seconds of indefinable happiness that make living worthwhile. And, like in a library, my heart can take out the memories, any day, any night, even when their author no longer waits for me to take her to the school bus.

The Snow Bowl

It was Super Bowl time, and for my son and me, watching the game was a slam-bang ritual we'd shared ever since he could talk. I say "slam-bang" because we'd spend more time arguing about which team was best than actually watching the game, which is what he probably loved most about it. And with him, for those few precious hours, I was ten years old again. So I often wondered: who enjoyed it the most?

As most of the world knows, the Super Bowl is typically played on the last Sunday in January. And, while the game may be played in ninety-degree California or Florida sunshine, or in a domed stadium, the snow's piled ten feet high in Montreal.

While millions tune in to watch the big game, only Jeremy and I know where the *really* big game is played. It's not called the Super Bowl, and there's no money at stake. If you want a glimpse of Heaven, though, then stop by one year to watch. Just make sure you're dressed for the North Pole. On the Saturday before the Super Bowl, my son and I play what we call "The Snow Bowl." And this year's game turned out to be the best one ever.

Jeremy was ten, and full of enough energy to match a dozen kids. Sometimes I wish there were more of me, just so I could keep up with my son.

It was a typical January afternoon: very cold, with mountains of snow, and a brisk, chilling wind.

"C'mon, Dad," Jeremy said. "It's almost 3:30. We'd better get the Snow Bowl started." At that point, I was so comfortable that only Jeremy and our Big Game could make me come out of hibernation. But every year we played, every catch Jeremy made and every smile on his face were better than the year before.

The rules were simple. We each picked our favorite National Football League team (not necessarily the ones in the Super Bowl). I'd play quarterback for both teams, while Jeremy made all the diving catches over the eight-foot mountains in our front yard. Each catch was worth five points. When it got dark, the team with the most points would be the winner. This year, we picked the New York Giants and the Tennessee Titans.

There wasn't a soul in the street when we started. It was a moment I wished I could freeze in time. I'd call the count, go back, evade a few attackers and let the bomb go. With each pass, I switched teams. I think Jeremy could have joined the circus with the acrobatic catches he made that day.

After almost an hour, our fingers became numb, our eyelashes were caked in snowflakes, and our toes seemed to have disappeared. Welcome to the Snow Bowl! By this time, we were making so much noise and having so much fun that some of the neighbors came out to cheer us on. Brave souls!

It was starting to get dark. The score was 70-60, in favor of the Titans. Within the next five minutes, the Giants caught up. What a game! It was now 70-70, with just minutes to go. ABC Sports, eat your heart out!

Because we'd both reached what we called the "ice cube point," we agreed that after two more passes, we'd call it a day. We started to talk it up, driving the excitement level to new heights. Even the people watching us began getting excited.

I threw the first pass for the Giants. It was a bad pass. This was it, then—the last pass, the last play. It all came down to this moment.

"Are you ready, Jeremy?" I shouted.

"Fire away, Pops!" he yelled. I purposely tried to make it at least a little difficult. In the corner of the yard, where Jeremy stood on top of a mountain of snow, there was a gigantic tree. I aimed the ball through the branches. For Jeremy to catch this one would have really been miraculous. I slowly called the signals, and then let the ball go. It went exactly where I'd aimed.

Jeremy wasn't fooled by my move. He followed the ball. As it swept through the branches, he made a diving catch as he disappeared over the mountain. I waited breathlessly for a second to see what had happened. Then, in a flash, Jeremy held up the ball.

"I caught it! I caught it, Pops. It's a miracle! I won! The Titans won!" I knew instantly that the catch wasn't a miracle. The smile on his face was the miracle.

"Time to go in, Jeremy," I said.

"I had the best time, Pops," he said. He gave me a big hug, and all of a sudden, I wasn't cold anymore.

My Summer Valentine

All my life, I've celebrated Valentine's Day. When I was younger, I loved it because it was the first holiday after Christmas. When I was a teenager, I loved it because it was my best shot at getting a date with the girl I dreamed about. When I went to university, most girls thought it was a dumb holiday, dreamed up by someone in the attic at Hallmark. When I got married, Laure and I always made a big deal about it.

But the best Valentine's Day I ever had didn't even happen on February 14. And I never got a card – not a kiss – not even a phone call. And to this day, nobody, not even my own family, knows—especially the one who made it a Valentine's Day I'll treasure forever.

It was a day that started out like most other workdays for me, and I imagine for most of the world. I got up early, reviewed my day's agenda, grabbed my coffee, jumped in the car, and headed off to my office. As I stopped at a red light, I took out my Blackberry email messenger to check and see, as I do about a hundred times a day, if I had yet received any emails.

By mistake—or maybe it wasn't a mistake— I hit the wrong button and ended up in the "task" section, which showed the number "2." That seemed odd to me, because I basically used my Blackberry to send and receive emails. The number "1" was for notes I wrote to myself as reminders. But where did the "2" come from?

Well, when I entered that number, it stopped me in my tracks, changed my day, and changed me forever. Whatever I was going to do that day, I didn't. I couldn't. Whatever I was thinking at that moment, I forgot. It didn't matter.

Over and over again, I read the second task. I must have read it a hundred times. Other drivers started to honk at me. I was still sitting at the red light, which had already changed to green and back several times, holding up traffic. I pulled my car to the side. I couldn't drive, at least not at the moment. I turned off the radio. I didn't want any distractions.

That second task was a Valentine's wish from my daughter Jenna. She'd probably forgotten she'd written it for me six months ago. Now, on an August morning, sitting in my car, I'd stumbled across it.

It read:

"I love u daddy!!!!!!!!!!!!!!!!! Happy Valentine's Day !!!!!!!!!!!!
Roses are red,
Violets are heather,
Tell me you love me,
Now and forever."

It was signed, *"Love, Your Princess."*

Now, whenever I feel a little low, or need to be reminded about what really matters, I take out my Blackberry, turn to task number "2" and the biggest smile in the universe covers my face. Shhhhh. Don't tell anyone. It's our secret—Jenna's and mine.

A Family Affair

As my kids get older, I find it's harder to come up with things to do as a family. I have to think more and plan more to ensure that days and months don't pass without spending time with them. It's so easy to believe it all will last forever, but it doesn't. All too soon, they'll be gone.

So, one weekend, I decided we were going to do something we hadn't done in a long time as a family—see a movie. These days it's hard to find a film the whole family could enjoy, but I finally picked one. That's when the resistance movement got underway.

Laure, my wife, was exhausted and would just as soon have stayed home. Jeremy, my thirteen-year-old son, wasn't sure if the movie I picked was edgy enough for him. If it was a movie the whole family could see, he figured it would probably be boring. Jenna, my eleven-year-old daughter, didn't care. She, like me, just wanted to do something as a family.

My battle to convince my troops ended quickly. We were going to the same movie at the same time, something of a rarity for a family with kids exploding on the teenage scene. I couldn't remember the last time we went to a movie together. On the way to the theater, Laure and the kids rattled on and on about what seemed like a thousand different subjects, none lasting more than about ten seconds.

Snapshots of Heaven

I heard everything and I heard nothing. I was lost in my thoughts, trying to figure out what was bothering me. Finally, I figured out my dilemma. True, we were going somewhere together, but we really wouldn't be together. What kind of family outing is this, I thought, where for two hours we sit in the dark and nobody says a word?

I was beginning to have nagging doubts about the whole idea. Why did I suggest a movie? What was I thinking? I was just about to turn around and go back home when Jeremy said, "You know what, Pops? I think it's a good idea for the whole family to go to a movie." Like clockwork, Jenna jumped in, echoing here brother's comment. So, end of dilemma. Movie, here we come.

Carrying popcorn, drinks, and candy, we made it our seats just as the lights dimmed. This was the second time I'd seen this movie, a rarity for me, but it was the only one we could all agree on. Halfway through, I began watching my kids watch the movie. My eyes began to dart back and forth like a ping-pong ball. What was the real show, I thought? No words were spoken. We had no eye contact and yet their faces, for me, became the showstopper.

I don't remember watching the rest of the movie. All the great scenes, costumes, and acting suddenly disappeared. As far as I was concerned, the real stars weren't the actors on the screen, but those two young people sitting beside me.

On the ride home, our car was transformed into a beehive of talk. Each of us became a critic. Imagine four critics talking at once, not listening to anyone else's opinion. It was wild, but it was fun wild. I loved it. I couldn't remember so much talk between us. It was clear that the movie was a hit, at least to our family. We erased the memory of two hours of silence in less than ten minutes. It was wonderful.

Like a kid in a candy shop, I grabbed onto every word, and ate it up. It was perhaps the only occasion in my life when I was so happy listening to people all speak at the same time, none finishing a sentence, but making more sense than I had ever heard.

Until that night, I always felt to be a family you had to do something together, talk together, go to an amusement park, or review each other's life over dinner. But that night, I learned you always have to be a detective of love. Clues are everywhere, you just have to look. I learned that you can do absolutely nothing together, not utter a word, not even a smile, and still have the time of your life—your family life.

124

The Magic Carpet Ride on Wheels

L eave it to my wife, Laure, to come up with a vacation idea that could both excite and bewilder anyone, even a Tibetan monk. And leave it to her to suggest the idea moments before we ended an exhausting work day.

"Michael," she said, just as I was settling into bed, "I have a great idea for a summer vacation." For a few seconds, I pretended not to hear. "Why don't we rent a motor home for a week?"

Looking straight into her eyes, I yelled, "Are you crazy? Us? Our family? Renting a motor home? We don't even own a tent! We can't go ten miles without a roadside Hilton! You can't be serious, Laure."

She was serious. Very serious! I continued ranting for a few minutes, then she did it. She always saves the best for last, setting me up perfectly like a set of bowling pins, then tossing the perfect strike.

"The kids will love it, Michael," she said softly. "It will be the adventure of a lifetime. They'll get a real kick out of it. Never mind you, think of them."

"That's not fair," I said. "Now you're fighting dirty." We both laughed and said goodnight. I never told her, but I was awake all night, having nightmares of being eaten alive by mosquitoes, smelling the septic tank back up into our RV, and paying hundreds of dollars for these unique experiences.

Summer rolled around and finally the day came when the kids and I picked up the RV. They excitedly ran around what would be their home for the next week, fighting over who'd get the top bunk bed.

A few hours later, we pulled out of our driveway and headed for Quebec City. Laure had made reservations for all the campsites, but we didn't anticipate one problem. When we finally arrived at the site, it was 3:00 a.m., but we quickly discovered that it closed at midnight. We parked outside the gate and fell asleep hours later, listening to the rain beating against our new home.

The next morning, there was a knock at the door. Surprise! A man handed me a $100 ticket, explaining that we were illegally parked and had never showed up for our reserved spot on the campground. At that moment, all I wanted to do was go home. But one look at my wife and kids told me they were in it for the long haul.

We started driving again. We arrived at the next campsite with plenty of time to relax, build a fire, and have a barbecue. We met a whole new world of people and actually started to have fun. It was like we'd slipped into a parallel universe where people become addicted to a whole different lifestyle. Each site is like a summer camp, with a swimming pool, a park, and a central hall where adults play Bingo and kids buy candy. Nights were spent playing board games, meeting neighbors, and listening to them play guitar by the campfire.

But, after three-and-a-half days of nonstop travel, I suggested we find a place to sit out the rest of the week. Laure and the kids agreed, so we headed for Granby, Quebec, which supposedly had the best camp-site for kids within a 500-mile radius. Granby didn't disappoint and, for me, the real vacation began.

There were rides, pools, games, and hundreds of other children. There was nothing but sunshine and eighty-degree weather everyday. We all loved every minute of it.

It was a great time for us as a family. But it was also the first time I saw my nine-year-old son begin to go off on his own, getting his first taste of independence. Every morning, Jeremy would head off by himself for the giant trampoline, and jump and jump, as if he were trying to touch the sky. Then he was off to the shuffleboard courts, where he found lots of new friends, kids his own age.

Ironically, this family outing we'd planned, and which we'd all enjoyed so much as a family, had taken on a new and somewhat unex-

126

pected dimension—my son was growing up, and beginning to test his wings.

For seven days we lived in a world we never knew existed. We did things we never did before. Visited places we never imagined - thanks to an RV that only minutes into the ride, I had regretted renting. Like the magic carpet in Aladdin, the RV swept us into a family adventure we would never forget. As we drove home Saturday night, I realized this vacation would quickly become one of our most important journeys. Reminding me like Aladdin's magic carpet that it was not and it never is the destination that matters, it's the experience, the magic carpet ride!

My wife's prediction that, "The kids will love it.... They'll get a real kick out of it," had come true. Jenna and Jeremy will never forget "The Magic Carpet Ride," and neither will Laure and I. For our family, stopping and staying awhile in Granby is filed in our memory bank under "Snapshots of Heaven."

A Basketball Game at Dawn

It took me years to discover that for all my son Jeremy's boundless energy, it takes less than five seconds for him to fall asleep. Once he's in Dreamland, a meteor hitting the earth couldn't wake him.

My daughter Jenna is the exact opposite. If my wife and I threw out the curfew rules, she'd probably stay up all night. More often than not, she wakes up in the middle of the night and asks me to come and sleep beside her. My wife Laure always responds the same way: "There you go. Why do you let her talk you into it every time? Why don't you just say no?"

It's because I'm a sucker. But I know my wife is right. I tell myself I'm going to march right into Jenna's room and repeat Laure's advice word for word.

An hour later, I rejoin my wife. It's now 3:30 a.m. Laure, like most of the world, is deep into sleep. As I finally start to doze off, Jenna again walks again into our room. I look at the clock. It's now nearly 6:00 a.m.

Jenna started to talk. As the night began turning into dawn, I realized something was about to happen, something that hadn't happened before and probably wouldn't happen again.

"Daddy, I have a great idea," Jenna blurted out, her eyes beaming

"What is it?" I dared to ask, my eyes closing fast from only two hours of sleep. I anticipated something totally off the wall. It hit me that I was going to experience something I'd never forget. But nothing prepared me for what followed.

"Why don't we stay in our PJs and go outside to play basketball?"

"But it's Sunday Jenna and very early in the morning."

"Exactly! What a perfect time, Daddy. You don't have to go to the office, and it's too early to use the phone. Why not?"

I couldn't believe my ears. Everything she said made sense, and yet it was almost 6:00 a.m. on a hot, humid Sunday in July. I ignored reality and off we went.

The only sound that could be heard on that otherwise peaceful morning was the thunder of the basketball hitting the pavement and the backboard. It was eerie! All around us, it was more silent than a library. It seemed nobody in the world was awake except Jenna and me.

After we finished warming up, which Jenna often spends more time on than the actual game, she shouted at the top of her lungs that it was time to play. Now I knew I had to wake up fast.

It seemed to take forever to iron out the rules. Finally we agreed that I had to score from the foul line, and she could either shoot from wherever she wanted, or dribble in toward the basket, untouched of course.

Jenna took her shot ten feet from the basket and scored. One bull's-eye and you'd think she had just won the Lottery. I shot next and missed. She shot again and scored.

"Yes, yes, yes," she shouted!

At that point, I was exhausted from the heat and lack of sleep. Only her uncontrollable laughter kept me going. Imagine a ten-year-old girl with a mean case of the giggles at eight o'clock Sunday morning!

For nearly two hours, we both happily surrendered to the thrill of the experience. No final buzzer here. Instead, my wife appeared in the bedroom window. "What on earth are you doing?" she hollered. "You're waking up the whole neighborhood."

"Okay, Daddy," said Jenna. "Enough. Let's go inside. I'm hungry."

I'll never forget the smile on Jenna's face, and I know I'll never forget the pure happiness I felt on that very hot, humid Sunday morning in July.

A Date with
My Daughter

"I have a great idea, Daddy," Jenna told me excitedly. "Let's go out for dinner, just you and me."

"What about Mommy and Jeremy?" I asked with a puzzled look.

"Oh, don't worry about them," she answered. "I suggested Jeremy go to a movie with Mom, and he thought that was a great idea."

"And what did Mommy say?" I asked

"Oh, she doesn't know yet," Jenna replied

"I'd love to go for dinner with you, Jenna," I said, quickly jumping at the opportunity of spending an evening, or at least a few hours, with my daughter.

"Great idea, right, Dad?"

"Great idea," I said. "Jenna, you could tell me all the things that happened in school this week and I could tell you all the things that happened at the office. Oh, by the way, Jenna, I almost forgot to ask. Where do you want to go for dinner?"

"Chinese, of course, Daddy, and that could only mean our favorite Chinese restaurant in the world – Chung Mei."

Five o'clock finally rolled around. As soon as we started out the driveway, Jenna began to chatter away about what she was going to eat at Chung Mei.

Actually the best part of the restaurant was the owner, the lady after whom it's named. Mei is a beautiful, vivacious lady who could make the meanest and the nastiest customer crack a smile, and who always makes you feel at home.

But kids were her specialty. She always paid special attention to kids. I don't know how many she had, or what kind of mother she was, but she continually walked up and down her restaurant searching out the kids, and for that moment became everyone's Chinese grandmother.

When we walked in, she greeted Jenna with her usual hug and asked how the family was doing. When you stepped into her small and always crowded restaurant, you felt like you were greeting the Chinese relatives you never had, but wished you did.

Jenna ordered her usual won ton soup, spring roll, and small portion of fried noodles. For me, my eyes were always bigger than my stomach. I ordered for three and usually took home more than I ate.

As usual, the food started arriving within seconds. Even though it was early Saturday evening, you could almost imagine everything you order just sitting there in the kitchen, waiting for the waiter to grab it.

As my little lady and I began to eat and gab away, sharing smiles and laughs and asking each other all kinds of zany questions, I forgot where we were. We could have been anywhere. For the next half-hour, there was nobody in the world except Jenna and me. In truth, for those thirty minutes, nothing else mattered.

When I finally came back to reality, I noticed the line waiting for tables getting longer and longer, and the waiters coming around again and again, asking us if we wanted anything else. The whole restaurant was staring at us, with gigantic smiles on their faces. You knew what they were thinking. I guess they felt what I felt, only from a distance.

Jenna went to the bathroom and I asked for the bill. When she returned, her usual fortune cookie was waiting for her, courtesy of "Grandma" Mei.

As we said our goodbyes, I held Jenna's hand tightly. She then ran toward the car and yelled back. "Come on, Daddy, let's race. The first one to touch the car wins." Of course, she won. What could I do? The night was like our whole life running away too fast. I needed her to win, not for her but for me. I needed that once-in-a-lifetime look on

Jenna's face as she turned, smiling at me as she touched the car first. Never was I happier to lose.

I guess like most guys I'd had my share of dates, including great ones with my wife Laure. But when you go on a date with your daughter, it's not just a date. It's giggles, it's silly faces, and it's this unbelievably deep feeling in your heart that astounds you every second you see her looking at you—your precious little girl.

The Jewish Santa

"C'mon, Daddy, it's Christmas morning. How long do we have to wait until you're ready?" My kids kept screaming at me from the other end of our upstairs hallway, "What's taking you so long?"

"Hurry!" my wife joined in.

Every year, it's the same thing. Christmas morning, coffee's hot, Ella Fitzgerald's belting out, "Have a Holly Jolly Christmas," while gifts wait impatiently to be opened. Our seven-foot tree proudly stood tall covered with white lights, silver balls, and ornaments that told the story of our family from day one. Within minutes, this peaceful scene would be transformed by a wild unwrapping frenzy, with colorful paper, ribbons, and delicate bows flying all over the room at a thousand miles a second. Nobody would know what to open first.

Within about five seconds, I was downstairs, yelling to everyone: "What's taking you so long?" Sounding like a herd of elephants, the kids zoomed downstairs, barely noticing me, and just about knocking over the tree.

My wife, in her usual role as MC, instructed me to get a garbage bag, so we all wouldn't drown in the sea of ripped paper that was about to fall like a Fourth of July celebration. Chaos ensued—but it was fun chaos. With the music blasting, the phone ringing every twenty min-

137

utes, and everyone talking, or rather screaming, at the same time, it was quite a sight. But it was a typical Christmas morning in our house, and I had almost as much fun as my kids.

Being Jewish and my wife Catholic, we celebrated all the major holidays. The kids were brought up Jewish, but I made sure we all went as a family to Midnight Mass on Christmas Eve and services on Easter Sunday. On all the major Jewish holidays, we went to the synagogue as a family, because at the end of the day, what mattered most was that we were always a family. And we always gave each other all that really mattered—and that was love.

Every year, our Chanukah/Christmas party was the social highlight of our community. Our Jewish friends couldn't wait to show their kids their only glimpse of a Christmas tree, and our non-Jewish friends were dazzled by the lighting of the menorah and watching us spin the dreidel.

My wife inaugurated an annual gift exchange, which became the high point of the evening. Everybody brought their kids. The hours flew by and, as always, everyone had the time of their lives and left with what I'm sure were many stories to tell. The next day the phone rang off the hook with "Thank-yous."

"I can't wait until your party next year, Laure," everyone said, as they wished her a great holiday.

"Tell me, Laure," I asked, "Do they ever say anything about me?"

"Absolutely," she said.

I suddenly got excited. "Really? What do they say?"

"You sure you want to know?" she asked.

"Of course!" What else could I say?

"OK. They all say, tell the Jewish Santa to also have a great holiday."

"The Jewish Santa! Is that what they call me?"

"That's it," said Laure.

But how do they know?

I immediately ran up stairs and yelled for my kids, "Jenna? Jeremy? What did you tell your friends about me?"

My SNAPSHOT of HEAVEN

WRITE YOUR OWN
SPECIAL OCCASION MOMENT

My SNAPSHOT
of HEAVEN

Snapshots of Heaven

Section Three:
Growing Up

"A child enters your home and makes so much noise that you can hardly stand it, then departs, leaving your house so silent that you think you will go mad."

John Andrew Holmes (1874-?)

When They Were Young

Every parent has the same hot flashes; the mind and heart go into warp speed, back in time. In seconds, you enter an emotional time tunnel, tumbling and bouncing from memory to memory.

Maybe it's because of our need to hold onto something lasting, in a world that changes by the techno-second, or maybe it's because we need that moment to escape to a land of permanent smiles.

I don't often drift back into my children's past. I don't even watch videos of the times when Jeremy and Jenna were younger. I'm not ready yet to watch yesterday. However, I have my moments when I have no choice. I need to go back! Someone or something always triggers my memories, and once they start, they don't stop. You can't just have one memory; you have to recreate months or years at a time.

On this afternoon, little did I know, but I was about to embark on a long flight into the past, and with the most unsuspecting person of all, my daughter. As we went around and around during a free-skating session, holding hands and laughing aloud, she started to pump me about when she and her brother were born, and how they were born, and what happened in their lives in the first few years.

It was hard for me. I was trying to keep my mind on the moment, savoring my luck. My daughter pushed on with the past as we skated around and around. Each turn brought a new story. We were no longer

147

on the ice; we were really in a time machine. Jenna had succeeded again in turning it backward.

She took me back to times I'd hoped would never stop, back to when I first ran endlessly with her up and down the street, teaching her how to ride her first two-wheeler. Her flashing smile took me even further back, to her first birthday party, when the sun poured its rays down on her, wearing that spectacular little dress and the hat with daisies on it. It was a scene I'll never forget! It was almost as if the sun itself knew she was the star of the day, a precious one-year-old gift from Heaven.

Jenna also helped me see what I couldn't see without her, that nothing was impossible, and that there's more good in the world than there is bad.

Bang! I hit the ice with a thud. Jenna was next to me in seconds, asking if I was hurt. Then, without waiting for an answer, she kept the questions coming. "Did you first want a son or a daughter, Daddy? Do you remember all those beautiful dresses you bought me when you traveled a lot? What was the craziest thing Jeremy ever did?"

Jenna knew the code that unlocks the photo album in my mind. No, I stand corrected. The album's not in my mind but in my heart. The pages fluttered in the wind of her words. The months and the years flew by in that hour of skating, almost as they do in real life. I realized then that if you're going to relive memories of your children, the best people to do it with are your children. It's as if you stand on the edge of the past, skating as we did around the memories, but never actually entering. I guess it's because you're busy creating new memories.

Funny thing about memories – they don't consume you, as long as you're living new ones. It's when you stand still that you get into emotional trouble. When parents have these round-robin discussions of when they were young, I've always avoided them.

The blaring siren in the arena signaled that our skating time was over. But that happy time with Jenna made me appreciate the fact that there is no time machine, and that memories with my children happen all the time. They never stop. Skating with Jenna made me realize my kids would always be young, at least to me. They would always give me memories that would take me to heaven before my time. And no siren could ever bring it to an end.

148

A Time to Let Go

One of my most harried experiences in raising my kids was teaching them how to ride a bike. I loved bikes, until I ran panting out of breath down the street, feeling I was on the verge of being admitted to the ER department of the local hospital. If I ever had any illusions about being in shape, they were shattered one minute into running alongside my kids. And if flirting with near exhaustion wasn't enough, my nerves were shot wondering when I'd slip up and they'd tumble to the ground, with skinned knees, elbows, or worse.

I know I was getting carried away with all this bike business, but it was taking a toll on me. When my kids were born, I dreamed of this moment, when I'd chalk up another great memory we'd all cherish forever. The only thing I wanted now was rain or foul weather. I never thought it would happen, but I prayed for bad weather.

My journey into parental breakdown was getting worse each time I went out, but I kept a smile on my face. This was supposed to be fun. It was to be a once-in-a-lifetime experience. I had to enjoy it. So, even if my lungs were bursting and I was shaking like a leaf, I loved it—I kept telling myself.

On the plus side, my career in bike training was near an end, and my body and mind were more or less intact. Jeremy had been riding for

149

more than two years, while Jenna was just about there, needing only a few more practice runs.

"Daddy, Daddy," she yelled from downstairs, "are you in the mood to go out and practice with me?" Honestly I wasn't. The air was so cold and damp that if anyone else on earth would have asked me the same question, and I mean anyone, the answer would have been a loud resounding "no." But Jenna asked, and she was almost there. I didn't want to stop now, with winter only days away. Who knew? With our luck, we could have twenty inches of snow by morning. What better thing to do than set out to live another memory, I thought, another adventure to store in our memory bank.

"C'mon, Daddy, hurry up. Let's go." The general was giving orders. I was only there for the ride. You'd think, with all the fancy, super-advanced gadgets we have today, someone could come up with a painless way to teach your kid how to ride a bike. But I guess, even if someone did, it wouldn't be the same. All the suspense and thrill would be gone.

"C'mon, Daddy," she shouted again. A few minutes later, Jenna and I were racing up and down the street. With each ride, I noticed she really was almost there.

"Should I let go?" I asked her, as we were halfway down the street.

"No, Daddy. I'm not ready yet."

"Remember what I told you, Jenna?"

"Yes, Daddy, I know there's never a right time."

"That's right, Jenna. You just have to go for it. You can do it. Believe in yourself. I'm going to let go."

"No, Daddy, not yet. I might fall and hurt myself."

"You might, Jenna, but that's the chance you have to take."

I guess my words hit home. Suddenly, she started pedaling faster and faster, and I could hardly keep up. Then she yelled, "Daddy, Daddy, let go! I've got it! I'm okay! Don't worry!"

Should I let go? Despite all my encouraging words, I wasn't sure what to do. What if she fell and hurt herself badly?

Then, as happens so often in my life, the answer just came. I let go. And she flew. On her own, free to fly, like she was driving a chariot of the gods up to the stars. I watched her race off to the end of the street and start back. Seeing the excitement and joy on her face, I was so thrilled for my little girl.

My mission had been accomplished, so why were there tears in my eyes? Maybe it was just from the cold, or maybe it was realizing this was only the first of many times when I'd have to let my daughter go. But I wasn't ready to do that—and I know I won't be ready tomorrow. Maybe I'll never be, even though I know the time is coming when I'll have to.

As we raced together to tell her mother the good news, I realized it was okay to feel this way. Perhaps one day I'll be able to say, "Go, Jenna. It's time to discover life on your own." But in my heart, I'll never let her go.

Gone Are
the Carpools

The night of Jeremy's graduation from elementary school still sticks in my mind, like it was yesterday. As I watched him and his friends go up to the podium to receive their diplomas, and listened to the school principal's speech about how they had their whole lives ahead of them, I sat quietly among the hundreds of parents, wondering why he had to go on to the seventh grade. Why couldn't he stay in the sixth grade forever? After all, we were having so much fun.

I started to remember when I first carpooled Jeremy and his friends Zac, Adam, and Catherine. Sometimes, one of them would cry when I picked them up. They never said very much on the drive to school. I guess they were still trying to wake up. I often tried to start a conversation, but most of the time I got the silent treatment. This, by the way, soon became one of the traditions of my carpool.

The other tradition was that, on the last day of every school year, I took the kids for a couple of hours to do something special. In the first few years, we used to go for ice cream or to everyone's favorite candy store, where they'd stuff their pockets. Later, I'd get calls from their parents wondering what I had done.

My favorite end-of-school experience was when they finished fifth grade. It was an unusually hot June day. Scorching hot! So hot you could fry bacon on a car. We were all wondering what to do this year,

153

but I warned them I had less time than usual because I had to rush back to a meeting. I was always checking my watch while I was bringing them to and from school, to ensure that I wouldn't miss too much work.

As we were searching for something to do, we passed a small wading pool. "Let's go into the pool," Zac said.

"Yeah, let's," they all echoed. The idea started to catch on like a forest fire.

"You guys are crazy," I said. "First of all, you don't have your bathing suits and, second, I have no time."

"Oh, c'mon, it will be a blast," Adam said.

And then my son Jeremy came in for the kill. "C'mon, Daddy. Never mind the office. Wouldn't you rather do this?"

What could I say? At that moment, my thoughts went back in time to when I finished fifth grade. I stopped the car—ordered everyone out and into the pool. Before the words were out of my mouth, they were already in the water.

Almost an hour went by before I realized what I'd done. The kids had the time of their lives. We were all soaking wet as I drove them home, and they couldn't stop laughing. No parent ever called, but I could imagine the words that were said about me.

Laure shook me. "Wake up! Wake up! It's Jeremy's turn to go to the podium. He looks so handsome! I can't believe he's going to be in seventh grade already. Quick, get the camera. Here, let me take the pictures."

When Jeremy came over to us afterward to give us a hug, I whispered in his ear, "Want to go swimming?"

He smiled. "Carpool's over, Daddy."

"I guess you're right, Jeremy." Then he ran to talk with his friends.

Actually, that same wading pool we'd been in two years earlier was only a mile away. It was June and the temperature was over eighty. I was ready to go in. Funny, I was now the only one who was. But that's okay. It's stored forever in my memory bank and, whenever I want I can go back and relive that happy moment in my mind.

The Breakfast Battle

It's Sunday morning at 7:30. I crawl out of bed, my eyes barely open, and yell across the hall toward our TV room.

"Jenna? Jeremy? Do you want to go to the diner for breakfast?" No answer. Much louder this time: "Jenna? Jeremy? Do you want to go out for breakfast?"

Still no answer. Either I'm speaking (or yelling) a foreign language, or my kids have disappeared and have been replaced by two green Martians. And so begins Breakfast Battle #789.

It's now 7:45. The great tranquility of Sunday morning enjoyed by the rest of the world has become another fantasy in our house. By now, I've incurred the wrath of my wife for waking her up at such an ungodly hour. She gets up, staring at me in disbelief.

"Are you going to yell at the kids all morning, or are you going for breakfast?" she asks. "Maybe they don't want to go. Maybe they don't care." This was all I needed. My wife had once again pushed my hot button. These kids were going for breakfast! I knew they loved it, once they got going. I just had to jump-start the process.

I go to Jenna first. She's my biggest fan, at least when it comes to Sunday morning breakfasts.

"Sure, Daddy, I'd love to go," she says, her eyes intently gazing at the television. Like a skillful Henry Kissinger, I then move to Jeremy, who always has to be delicately pushed along.

"No, Dad," he says, as usual. "I'm not in the mood. You can bring it back if you like." I turn to my ally for help, and wink.

"C'mon, Jerm," she blurts out. "We'll sit at the counter and talk and talk and talk."

An hour later, the debate comes to an end. We all get dressed and off we go. The second we enter the car, Jenna and Jeremy start chattering simultaneously, putting the battle on hold. Thankfully, the diner is only four minutes from our house.

Entering the place is like traveling fifty years back in time. The tables, the chairs, the walls—everything about the place is old. The second you turn its revolving doors, you practically bump into Aunt Delilah behind the counter. It seems like she's been there forever. I don't know if she has any children but she certainly loves mine.

Whenever she sees Jenna and Jeremy, she laughs. Since they were babies, she's watched them fight for the best counter seats. You'd think she had ringside seats to the game of the century, the way she revels in their monthly counter duels, as they battle for position.

Jenna orders her first apple juice, a bowl of cereal, and a double order of toast. Jenna never eats the crusts, letting them pile up toward the sky. Jeremy orders his favorite. First, he'll have one of five glasses of apple juice, an omelet with bacon (we always fight over how much bacon he orders), and a double order of burnt white toast (his dad's favorite).

While we wait for our food, Jenna rattles off about each day at school in the past week. I love listening to her—it's my chance to catch up. But when I turn to Jeremy to ask about his week, Jenna keeps right on talking, and the battle is on. That's why I always sit between them. If I didn't, we'd have probably been thrown out a long time ago.

Thankfully, the food comes fast. Jeremy finishes in record speed, and is ready to leave. Jenna, on the other hand, likes to take her time. It's now almost 10:00 a.m. and the chaos continues. While much of the world, between the ages of fifteen and forty-five, is still not awake, we've spent the morning hopping along a dozen counter stools, made three trips to the bathroom, and chatted with about seven people we've never met.

At this point, it's time to go. Everyone has had enough. Jeremy thanks me, and reminds me that he has a lot of fun with me. Then, as we leave, Jenna takes my hand. Message received. The battle is over. There have been no casualties. All is well!

So Busy Being Busy

B ang! It's first thing Monday morning. My office door opens and closes faster than the speed of light, as my friend Marilyn charges in. I'm still trying to shake off the weekend cobwebs, and not anywhere close to my work mode. Marilyn says she's ready to scream and needs someone to talk to.

"Do you realize what I did this weekend?" she asked. "It was my first business trip to New York. I was taking an early flight so I decided to pack the night before. I'd be away for two nights. As I was packing, I began thinking how much I'd miss my husband and my daughter Jessica, who just turned two. This was to be the very first time I'd leave her for more than a day."

"As I packed, my emotions got the best of me and tears sprung to my eyes. I was going to miss her so much. Did this ever happen to you?"

"All the time," I said.

"How do you deal with it?" she asked, but before I could answer, she continued. "You know I'm a very emotional person and every once in awhile I get scared that something could happen to change my world. What if something happened to me? Who'll tell Jessica how I really feel about her? My husband could try, but it just wouldn't be the same.

159

"I decided it was time to complete Jessica's baby book. It's called 'How Much I Love You,' and chronicles the first two years of her life. Her birthday had just passed, so it was time to finish the last few pages. In the back of the book, there are pages for notes. I opened the book to a fresh page and started to write."

"You see, the most important thing I could do for my daughter is to make sure that no matter what happened to me, she'd always know exactly how much she's loved. That would be my forever gift to her, for all the hundreds of gifts and lessons she's already taught me in her short two years on earth."

"I want Jessica to know she's the air I breathe, that I'm so proud of the little toddler she's become. Not a day goes by that I don't get tears of joy in my eyes. She's like a big warm hug! I told her I felt the same about my kids and suspected parents everywhere did too."

"Then," she said quietly, "Jessica has managed to teach me about life. She's taught me to take one moment at a time, to enjoy all the minutes that make up a day. She's taught me to slow down, and enjoy things like a good book or movie. After all, her day is filled with books, toys, and videos. There's always time to play."

"My favorite part of the day is right after supper, when I sit and read and play with Jessica until bedtime. Evenings, when it's not too cold, we put her in a wagon and pull her around the neighborhood. She points and gives us the names of all the things she sees. Life is so simple at these times, and it just doesn't get better than this."

By this time, three people had knocked on my door and I already had four phone messages. "Oh," said Marilyn, "you're busy. I'll come back later."

"No," I said. "This is the best time for this. The rest can wait."

"I think the most important lesson Jessica has taught me in these two short years is that life is simple. We're the ones who complicate everything. We all need to slow down, to read, to play, and be happy."

She still hadn't said if she went to New York or not, so I interrupted her. "So what happened? Did you get up enough courage to go after all this?"

"Yes, of course. While I was sitting in the airport nervous and waiting impatiently, I realized I had no reason to rush. I was plenty early, so I opened up my travel case, glanced at the office files I brought, smiled and pulled out a book I've been meaning to read for a year. As I did, I silently thanked my daughter for reminding me to take the time to read, play, and be happy."

Suddenly, it was no longer Monday. Thanks to Marilyn, it already felt like Thursday. I couldn't wait to spend the weekend with my kids. Thanks to her, besides all she said about what her daughter taught her, the greatest gift was the reminder that even Monday mornings couldn't compete with the precious memories of the smiles and laughter of our kids.

I Don't Know You, Daddy!

It was a hot, humid Sunday afternoon in July. My daughter Jenna and I were riding our bikes, when I suddenly realized it doesn't get any better than this, and I spontaneously burst out singing. My inhibitions vanished.

Stopping my bike, I became what I'd always dreamed, the DJ of Grand Street, belting out favorite songs from my favorite time, the '60s, jumping from The Animals, to The Turtles, to The Lovin' Spoonful, to The Rolling Stones, and to The Beatles—singing the best for my best of times.

As if to challenge my singing supremacy, dogs started barking, cars began to honk in tune, and if that wasn't enough excitement, a little old lady interrupted her Sunday stroll, beating her cane on the sidewalk to the famous melody, "A Hard Day's Night."

Amidst this impromptu carnival, Jenna didn't move or say a word. Staring at me in disbelief, she finally blurted out, "What are you doing, Daddy? What are you doing? You are so embarrassing! I don't know you."

It caught me completely off guard. It was the first time my daughter ever told me I embarrassed her, let alone that she didn't want to know me. I was lost for words, something of a rarity for me.

163

All I could say was, "What did I do wrong?" I felt like I was defending myself in court.

"You mean you don't know, Daddy?" At first, I honestly didn't get it. But in a few seconds, it hit me. Oh, dear, I said to myself. My daughter has grown up to the point that now I can embarrass her. I'd never had to deal with this before. What kind of change is this between father and daughter? I was embarrassing her. What a strange new experience for a parent!

Finally, Jenna jumped on her bike, sped home, and occasionally looked back with that funny, irresistible, angry nine-year-old face that melted my heart. I raced after her, but not before thanking my audience and apologizing that I had to leave in such a hurry. One minute before we got to our house, I finally caught up to her, yelling what we always did as we got close to home: "First one to touch the garage door is the winner."

"You're on," she yelled back. Whether she knew it or not, I always let her win. She was still young enough for me to do that.

As we opened the garage door, Jenna asked me if, as a special treat, I'd pick her up from school the next day, but only if I promised not to embarrass her. What could I do? I put my hand up and promised. It was like being in court and putting your hand on the Bible before you testify.

The next afternoon finally rolled around. While I was driving to pick her up, I repeated the mantra, "I won't embarrass Jenna. I won't embarrass Jenna." Everything was fine; I was under control.

Then, as I got to the school, and started down the hallway to Jenna's homeroom, I lost it. I don't know why, but I forgot everything I'd promised her.

I looked over the heads of about a hundred screaming kids who couldn't wait to get out of the building, as books fell and locker doors slammed tight to end another day. I felt like the parent searching for his kid at a rock concert. In my trademark fashion, I started screaming, "Jenna, Jenna, Daddy's here, and I'm on time."

Out of the corner of my eye, I saw Jenna running into her classroom. When I caught up with her, all she could say was, "You promised, Daddy. You promised not to embarrass me!" I didn't know what to say.

As we walked to the car, I asked her how her day was. She was silent. As we drove away, all I could think of was how precious she looked and how lucky I was. I told her that I'd try to do better and not embarrass her. She was still, but now she smiled.

Somehow, having her tell me I embarrassed her really touched my heart. My precious little daughter was growing up. And I knew that someday, when she's a grown woman, it won't be my showing off that will embarrass her, but comments I might make about her clothes, or her makeup, or the company she keeps. But that's okay. I know she loves me, even when I embarrass her, and that's plenty good enough for me.

Love in Any Language

Ever notice how complicated things become as your kids get older? You struggle with them for everything, you argue over everything, and, worst of all, they don't want to spend time with you anymore. They'd rather be with their friends.

What is this? Their friends? My kids? Are they really at that age already? What happened? Something went by me quickly, but I never saw it. Was I like that? Impossible!

My wife has an easier time than I do watching our kids get older. As she says, she'll always have her memories. For me, it's unbearable. So like any creative parent, I've worked painstakingly over the years developing a kind of code between my kids and me.

Now that Jeremy's thirteen and Jenna's eleven, I know they don't want to say and do things they did when they were five or six. Who can blame them? I was the same way at that age. But I had to do something.

My biggest challenge is when I tell my kids I love them (which I do every day). I'm never sure how they'll respond. How do I get my kids to say, "I love you," as they get older, without actually saying it, but meaning the same thing? If bringing up a child is the biggest responsibility in life, the second biggest is keeping them close as the world intervenes.

167

My kids helped me create a world within our worlds, with new versions of "I love you, Daddy." My initial fear that they'd become too distant from me quickly faded as we together reinvented our relationship with one another.

Jeremy loves Coke, especially in the old-fashioned glass bottles. So do I. Whenever we can, we each buy one and drink them together. Eventually this became a kind of bond between my son and me. When he wants to tell me he loves me, he just says, "Two glass Cokes, Daddy, two glass Cokes." And I understand. He doesn't have to say anything else. These are our words, our unique language.

My daughter and I also have our own language. It's different than the one I have with Jeremy, and I'm sure it's very different than other fathers and daughters, yet the same. One of my favorites with Jenna is our milkshake kiss. I always used to tell her, and I still do, that I can't handle the fact that she's growing up so fast.

One night, she came up with a novel idea. "You know what, Daddy," she said, as I was about to kiss her goodnight. Let's start a new kiss."

"A new kiss," I exclaimed, caught off guard. "A new kiss? What kind of new kiss, Jenna?"

"What's your favorite thing at Dairy Queen, Daddy?"

I didn't understand what Dairy Queen had to do with a kiss and I said so. "C'mon, Daddy, just answer the question."

I caught myself and came back to her world. "I don't know."

"Of course you do," she said. "It's a milkshake, a chocolate milkshake."

"Okay, you're right. So?"

"That's it, the milkshake kiss," she said.

"And what's the milkshake kiss, Jenna?" I asked, as I started to laugh. She then showed me the way, as she has so many times in her life.

"Put your hand up, give me a high five, and then we shake our faces at each other."

"That's the milkshake kiss?" I asked.

"Yes, Daddy, that's the milkshake kiss. Do you like it?"

"Like it? Like it? I love it! Except you forgot one thing, Jenna."

"What's that, Daddy?"

"What's most important ingredient in a chocolate shake, Jenna?"

"The chocolate, Daddy?" She smiled, reached up, put her arms around and gave me the longest hug ever.

Over the years, I've learned that the language our kids use to say "I love you" changes as they grow up. What never changes is that we need to keep right on loving them, so they never stop giving us milkshake kisses and glass-bottled Cokes.

Ten Million Kisses

There's one thing about parenthood I'm learning fast—learning to wake up without my kids being in the next room. It's all about your kids moving more and more out the door as you helplessly watch, wishing Merlin would make them five forever.

I've just entered this phase. And like every new parent phase after your kids reach eight or so, it's agonizing. I know it's only summer camp or the grandparents' country house. It's no big deal. They're safe. They're with family. But already I don't like it. In time, they say, you can get used to almost anything. But not me.

From day one, I didn't understand. My mind and my heart were confused and lost by the eerie silence of our home without the kids around. It's funny sometimes, but I can hear myself in the past, yelling for them to quiet down. What I wouldn't give for a few yells now.

Not a day doesn't go by when, having dinner with my wife or alone, glancing out our kitchen windows, I don't imagine I see my son Jeremy doing his famous slam dunks. Maybe they'll never make him eligible to play for the Harlem Globetrotters, but to me they're the most awesome slam dunks in the world. I know it's crazy. I even know its part of a parent's life, the part I vow to fight.

My daughter Jenna, age eleven, went to stay with her grandparents in the country for a week. I was so happy for her—so unhappy for me.

171

Don't get me wrong. I love time alone with my wife Laure. But as the zebra can't hide its stripes, I can't hide my ache, the ache in my heart.

Twice a day, while she was away, Jenna and I spoke by phone. Same questions everyday, two times a day. "How was your day, Daddy?" "How was yours, Jenna?" "What's the weather like?" "What did you eat for supper, Jenna?"

These simple questions were poor disguises. The worst part of it all was never what I thought it would be. I always thought saying goodbye to Jenna at the end of each call would be the most difficult. I was wrong.

The worst part was not seeing her face. Not seeing her contagious smile. Not feeling her arms around my neck. I never saw it coming. I never understood, until now, just how much I needed hers, or Jeremy's, smile. But with Jeremy, I've yet to find out how hard it is, because his summer camp doesn't allow telephone calls unless it's an emergency.

Obviously, an aching parent heart doesn't qualify as an emergency. I laughed to myself thinking what it would be like if they allowed parent phone calls. The camp would grind to an abrupt halt. All day long counselors would do nothing but yell, "Johnny, phone call!" "Zac, it's your mother." "Brandon, your father's calling." "David, it's your grandmother."

So, with Jeremy, I never came face to face with the ache. I was left with only his letters, and my imagination hearing his words: "Pops, want to go out and shoot some baskets?" "Daddy, are you in the mood to play three on three?" I was always in the mood when he asked, even if I wasn't. Sometimes, the temperature soared over ninety degrees when he decided to race down court. My mind was thirteen, but my body never understood that.

What made my initiation into this new parent adventure even more difficult was having them both away at the same time. But, in some ways, the daily phone calls to Jenna helped make it a bit easier.

Fortunately, the week was finally coming to an end. In less than twenty-four hours, Jenna would be home. In less than twenty-four hours, the week away would be yesterday's news. In our final phone call, I said, "I'm going to give you ten million kisses, Jenna, when you come home."

She started to giggle. I loved it—and she knew it. "Did you hear me, Jenna? Ten million!"

"Yes, Daddy. I heard you. Me too, Daddy, me too."

With those words she sent me soaring through the clouds, and I didn't stop soaring until the minute she walked through the door. However, I didn't give her ten million kisses. I changed my mind. My heart threw in a bonus. I upped it to twenty million!

A Fare from the Heart

I t hit me like a blizzard. Only worse! Snow melts in real blizzards, but this one lasts for years. I was becoming a taxi driver for my kids—my next phase of parenthood.

I should have been prepared. They all warned me about the hours—about the demands—any time any day. But I wasn't. I wasn't ready then and I'm still not ready now. And yet somehow we find the way. We get by.

Once you hit the blizzard, there's no way out, at least not until your kids learn how to drive on their own. And who can even think such a thought at this point? My kids drive? I'd rather be on duty 24/7.

Often, when I'd drive my son Jeremy and his friends home from an evening event, words would fly out of their mouths that made me wish my ears would drop off. Where did they learn such things at thirteen? If I ask how their night was, I sometimes wonder if anyone heard me. In fact, I sometimes wondered if any of them, including my son, realized they were no longer at the party.

As you get deeper into the job, the whole thing becomes clear. It's not just about a few late party nights. No, not at all! This is just the beginning. The late party pickups lead into a barrage of events, functions, and classes you never in your wildest parental dreams thought existed.

175

How could kids go to all these things? Do they still go to school? When do they sleep or eat? The list is endless. Piano lessons. Ballet classes. Hockey practices. Soccer games. Preschool art, Mom and tot story time.

One year into my new profession, I was seeing my kids more inside the car than out. I worked, slept, ate, and drove a "cab," in what folks laughingly call "spare time." Truth be told, I was having trouble adjusting to my new taxi role. I never got it! What did kids do a hundred or even fifty years ago? Playing taxi driver wasn't turning out to be my favorite part of parenthood.

Then, one evening last summer, I learned to stop playing the role of taxi driver and was reminded of who I was. It was Mathew's father who reminded me. Mathew was Jeremy's friend, and they played tennis together on Friday nights. I didn't know his father very well. In fact, I didn't know him at all, except our paths would cross when we'd drive our sons to the tennis courts.

One Saturday night, I got to know him better than some people I'd known for years. As usual, I'd arrived a few minutes early to pick up Jeremy from a big bash that was ending around midnight. And, as usual, Mathew's father was already standing beside his car, watching the party going on in the backyard across the street. It then dawned on me that he was always very early, and always had a gigantic smile on his face. Many times before, I'd wanted to ask him why he came so early, but I hadn't. This time, I did.

"Father to father," I said, "why do you come so early? And why do you always have such a big smile on your face at such a late hour? Aren't you exhausted from playing taxi driver, like the rest of us? Don't you look forward to the day they drive themselves?"

"No," he said, "not at all. I love driving Mathew and his friends. I'm not his taxi driver. I'm his father. The reward for me is to be with my son and his friends and share these moments with him. It's my way of being with him, without being with him. Do you understand?"

"I'm starting to," I answered.

"I'd drive Mathew anywhere, anytime, forever. My fare is my heart. When he gets his license, these great times will be over. Gone! Another chapter closed!"

Seven months later, Mathew's father died instantly of a heart attack, at the age of fifty-three. Now, every time I drive my son or daughter anywhere, I always think hard about his words that night. My only regret is that I never got the chance to thank him. He was right. It is a fare from the heart.

Father Knows Best? Not Always!

From the day my son Jeremy was born, I always knew what to do as his father. But all that came to a crashing halt in the last six months as he grew faster than he'd grown over the last ten years. The confusing, beguiling, and frustrating years of a teenage son were just around the corner.

Back in the beginning, being a father came easy for me. From the second he opened his eyes, I decided Jeremy was destined to become a great lover of sports, like his dad. I filled his first bedroom with sports stuff—baseball bats and his first hockey skates. I couldn't wait to play with my son.

Over the years, I don't remember how many 7:00 a.m. hockey practices we just made, or how many hot dogs we ate at baseball games. I always knew what made him happy. We'd talk about every sports event and personality like we were writing the sports section for the local paper. I was proud of myself. I was there for my son. I always knew what to do!

Wasn't it only eight months ago when he turned six, calling me at the office asking when I was coming home to wrestle with him? How did we fall from doing high-fives at football games to him reminding me that I don't understand. What happened? Was it him entering high school that changed the rules? Or was it me forgetting I ever went to high school? Something had changed that much I knew. What had I missed?

I was at my wit's end. I couldn't sleep. I sat awake in the kitchen, where I always sought refuge. Finally, I figured it was time to call it a night. From the kitchen, I had to pass Jeremy's bedroom to get to ours. Then, for some reason, I decided to stop at his room. And I began to realize something. On the walls, on the tables, inside his CD player, was the story of Jeremy. Much of that story was with me, but not all. I pushed further, entering *his* world on my own.

There was the picture of Babe Ruth I gave him when he was six, plus boxes of baseball and hockey cards we'd collected, and that priceless picture of Sandy Koufax I bought him five years ago. He was so excited when he got it. Smiles covered my face as I traveled back with Jeremy to the times when I knew it all—or thought I did.

But then, I realized it didn't end there. There was more to my son. Inside his CD player were discs of singers I never heard of. And when he played them, I sometimes told him I didn't think that music could compare to my music of the Sixties.

Suddenly, I realized how wrong I'd been, how terribly wrong. For a second, I wanted to wake him and squeeze him so tight, but instead I kept looking for clues. I knew I was on to something. In the corner of his room were unrolled posters of his favorite rap stars. On his desk were DVDs of his favorite video games.

It was now 4:30 a.m. I sat staring at him, tears streaming down my cheeks. I got it! Finally, I understood that Jeremy was starting to take a different path. The answers were there all the time. I just had to look. I just had to open my heart. My son was growing fast. I was not.

"What are you doing?" My wife's voice startled me. "Do you know what time it is?"

"No," I said.

"It's 4:30 a.m. How long have you been here?"

"Since three, I said."

"Why?" But, as usual, Laure knew why. She always knew. "Come on to bed. You're going to be dead for work."

As I started to follow her out, I went back and gave Jeremy something he didn't like me to do much anymore, a great big kiss. To my shock, he momentarily opened his eyes, looked at me and said, "I love you, Pops. I love you very much."

180

"Me too, Jeremy. Me too!"

I practically ran to tell Laure. "I didn't want to tell you this before," she said. "I didn't think you were ready but I know you are now. Last night, as I kissed Jeremy goodnight, he asked me if I hurt myself. I was caught off guard. I didn't know what he meant. So I asked him. "When you fell from heaven, Mommy, did you hurt yourself?"

"What did you say?" I asked her.

"I just said no, then kissed him and walked out with tears in my eyes."

I knew what she meant. She was much better with the idea of Jeremy growing up than I was. She was giving him room to grow. I realized I could learn a lot from my wife and son.

That night I found the peace I'd been missing. I realized I didn't have to always know, that there wasn't a perfect formula, that like a road, I'd have to bend and follow the curves along the way. Jeremy's road was about to take different curves. I realized I had to take the curves with him, even if I didn't know where we were going. This was definitely going to be a great day.

My SNAPSHOT of HEAVEN

WRITE YOUR OWN
GROWING UP MOMENT

My SNAPSHOT
of HEAVEN

My SNAPSHOT
of HEAVEN

Check with your neighborhood and online book stores

Telephone orders: Call 1-866-37-CAMEO (372-2636) toll free. Have your credit card handy.

Secure Online Ordering: www.cameopublications.com

Postal Orders: Cameo Publications, PO Box 8006, Hilton Head Island, SC 29938-8006, USA. Tele: 843-785-3770